The Lurcher

The Lurcher

TRAINING AND HUNTING

Frank Sheardown

SWAN·HILL
PRESS

First published in the UK in 1996
by Swan Hill Press, an imprint of Airlife Publishing Ltd

British Library Cataloguing in Publication Data
    A catalogue record for this book
    is available from the British Library

ISBN 1 85310 830 8

Typeset by R. H. Services, Welwyn, Hertfordshire
Printed in England by Biddles Ltd, Guildford and King's Lynn.

Photographs: Ian Johnson and Frank Sheardown

Swan Hill Press
an imprint of Airlife Publishing Ltd
101 Longden Road, Shrewsbury SY3 9EB, England

Contents

Introduction

Many years ago when I was a boy, Greyhounds were Greyhounds, Whippets were Whippets and any other sort of a running dog was a lurcher, such things as Borzois and Afghans never having been seen in my neck of the woods. Today things have altered and running dogs are now usually divided between lurchers and longdogs.

Just to keep the record straight here are my own definitions. The **longdog** is either a purebred Greyhound, Whippet, Deerhound, Wolfhound, Borzoi, Saluki, Afghan Hound, Sloughi, a cross between any of these pure breeds, or a cross between their crosses, until such time as blood other than longdog is introduced. A **lurcher** is a crossbred between any longdog and a breed other than longdog. It is the lurcher that this book is all about.

In the main it is about those dogs which are produced as the result of matings between Greyhounds or Whippets and gundogs, guard dogs, sheepdogs and terriers with a few other sorts thrown in for good measure.

Frank Sheardown 1996

— 1 —
History of the Lurcher

The lurcher from centuries gone by, and even some of the best ones that I have known in more recent times, would be unlikely to be placed in any class in one of today's lurcher shows. To the uninitiated some of them would not even appear to be lurchers but rather some sort of mongrels, a little longer in the leg perhaps than others of their kind but nonetheless mongrels. Even at the best of times appearances are apt to be deceptive and the true lurcher of old used to be a pretty deceptive sort of dog, a cunning dog, and one possessed of infinite guile. In this it was almost always matched by its equally crafty owner.

One of the most successful poachers that I ever encountered would have passed, as far as the uninformed onlooker might have been concerned, as some superior sort of butler, the sort that one might have expected to find in the household of an archbishop. His dog, though obviously of mixed blood, was respectable and innocuous in its appearance and demeanour. Also innocuous in its appearance was the highly polished walking stick which he habitually carried when out on his apparently respectable walks with his equally apparently respectable wife, but the cane had a two inch .410 cartridge in its breech and its silver band concealed a hidden trigger just as his wife's neat coat was equipped with many hidden pockets; she always seemed to be stouter on the way back home than she did when going out. Or so the frustrated gamekeepers who never managed to catch either of the couple with the goods on them used to say. As for the dog, it was a perfect model of decorous behaviour as it sniffed around the hedgerows, its sheeplike appearance alone displaying its Bedlington origins, and it never even barked.

This was one of the later examples of a type of dog which has been in existence for a very long time, in fact ever since it paid a man not to be too overt as to his hunting activities. How many centuries do we have to go back to arrive at the origins of the lurcher? No one knows the answer but they must have been with us ever since there have been Greyhounds and their kind, which takes us back to at least ancient Greece and Rome.

If we look back to the times in this country when the punitive Forest Laws were being enforced it becomes clear why the peasant was so reticent about his dog's ancestry and abilities. It was more than a poor man's life was worth to possess a dog which might in any way have been seen to be capable of pulling down any of the deer which abounded throughout the countryside. No shadow of doubt was allowed to exist that deer were the property of the aristocracy, in some cases royalty alone, and as such were afforded every protection from the ravages of the peasantry with their illegal dogs and bows and arrows, the peasantry's (to the Normans) less than satisfactory attitude being typified by the tales concerning such naughty fellows as Bold Robin and the Jovial Friar with his inordinate appetite for unlawful venison pastie.

In more recent times, although the laws were nowhere near so draconian, game still belonged to the wealthy landowners and their views on protecting it from the lower orders had not changed much since the times of their Norman ancestors. Cases were far from rare during the period between the two World Wars when farm tenants, let alone their workpeople, received their marching orders solely for owning a running dog. Such expulsions were dressed up under some other guise but everyone knew what it was all about and the true story behind it.

The Saxon peasant was no thick witted loon and although short on formal education must have been long on native cunning, his metabolism frequently being sharpened by the pangs of hunger. As well as the downtrodden Saxon there was also his Nordic cousin, who had settled on the lands of the North East, and who had to be even more cunning for the invading Normans as one of their earlier acts had completely laid waste all territory to the north of the Humber. What few remaining Celts there were happened to be survivors and for that matter still are.

It is probably from these early days that the lurcher originated, then as later betraying in its appearance as little of the sighthound as was possible. A far cry from the present day when we have an abundance of lurcher shows at which the honours usually go to those dogs which are the most sighthound like in conformation, and also when there are periodicals largely devoted to lurchers and their activities. Current thinking on the subject is only to be applauded but it must be remembered that today's lurcher is a totally different sort of animal from that of years gone by, just as the world it lives in is very different.

Lurchers of this less obvious variety were in existence during the days of my boyhood and are probably still to be found in some of the more rustic locations. Many a shepherd had a collie which seemed a bit long in the leg and such people usually seemed to attract rather a disproportionate part of the gamekeepers' time. In the part of the country where I lived there were a few independent farm workers still about, men who did not live in tied houses but who had a cottage and an acre or so, either their own freehold property or that of a nonfarming landlord. Some of them were the survivors of copyholders, the cottagers who had managed to survive the enclosures. They would work on farms as they pleased, a few days here and a few days there, taking mainly piecework but never when there were wildfowl about or when the salmon were running. At such times as this they were to be found in the vicinity of the river or the estuary, usually accompanied by their gundogs many of which seemed to be of rather a more racy build than would have found favour on the show bench, even in those days. If you were to enquire as to what they were you would be assured that the animal under discussion was a flatcoat or a curly coat or a water spaniel; 'Pure bred, thoo knowest. Came fra' owd Jonathon 'Urst o'er at Cottal 'All.' It always seemed to be of the late Jonathon Hurst's line whatever the reputed breed. Not that this amounted to much to anyone who knew anything about the late gentleman for he had lived at the turn of the eighteenth and nineteenth centuries not at Cottal Hall but at Goole Fields and was chiefly remembered for his Shorthorn bull, Jupiter, which he had broken to the saddle and for the pig which he had trained to point. But he had been a well-known local character and therefore a convenient name to quote.

From time to time we were visited by gypsies, sometimes passing through in their vardos, two or three of them together, and at other times in brightly painted flat carts, the latter coming from one of the neighbouring commons before these had been ruined by the rash of housing which later appeared on them and where in those days the gypsies camped at various seasons of the year. It was then that one often saw a running dog which might have been recognised as such today. Most of those which I recollect at a remove of 60 years were midway in size between a Whippet and a Greyhound, some being smooth coated and others rough. They did not hang about long enough for one to see much of them, usually walking or running beside or under the horse drawn vehicles of their owners. For the same reason I never saw any of them working and so cannot say whether they were good, bad or merely indifferent.

The only running dogs which I recollect having seen worked openly in those far off days, just after the first World War, were those which arrived with their owners from the coal mining districts around Thorne and Hatfield. We used to have a grand panoramic view of events from the hills, a spur of the Lincolnshire Edge, as they exercised the strong old hares which abounded on the warplands adjoining the River Trent. It was a spectacle well worth seeing for not only were the hares exercised but similarly also were the gamekeepers of the Normanby Estate as they pursued the poachers over the flat countryside. The whole cavalcade was usually seen to be departing the scene in the direction of Gunness Station. Whether anyone was caught or not must have depended to some extent on the punctuality of the trains and the fugitives' knowledge of the timetables.

The General arrived on our local scene about 1931 and was the first person that I had ever met who went in for using a lurcher legitimately. He took a large house with plenty of stabling up on the Wolds and started upon his quest to breed the perfect lurcher. After trying all sorts of combinations of sighthound crosses to other breeds, he at last pronounced himself satisfied that he had fulfilled his lifetime's ambition. At the time, in my teens, I was not encouraged by my tenant farming relatives to show too much interest in the General's researches, but I do know one thing about them and that was that the final product carried both Greyhound and Airedale blood though in what proportions I do not know. Probably three-quarter sighthound to a quarter terrier I would be inclined to guess. Although this might give some sort of indication of what makes a good lurcher it is as well to bear in mind that this epitome of dogdom was what suited the General, what suited the country over which it was worked and what suited the times, the 1930s. For a lurcher is very much a dog of its time, altering in its makeup to suit the time, the place and the person.

Recently a great deal has been written about the so called Smithfield collie and its part in the creation of the modern lurcher. I think this should be treated with some caution and taken as only one possible strand in the tangled web of the lurcher's history. I have serious doubts as to whether the Smithfield ever existed as a breed in its own right. It should be remembered that Smithfield as the name of a cattle market was not confined to that part of the world in the City of London with Bart's Hospital and the Bishop's Finger alongside it. There were Smithfields all over the country and it seems to me to be more than likely that any sort of dog which took livestock to any one of them would be called a Smithfield in one place, a drover's dog in another and a sheepdog or cattledog elsewhere. This point concerning the Smithfield perhaps underlines one of the major problems in tracing the history of most breeds or types. It is only in recent times, since the advent of dog shows in the latter part of the last century, that many of the breeds we know have been fixed. Before this time breeds and types were continually changing, the criteria being ability to do the job rather than looks, and what today would be considered cross breeding was commonplace. The Greyhound in fact is very unusual in having such a long and well documented history and we should not mislead ourselves into thinking that particular breeds of collie or gundog were universally available to our ancestors for creating lurchers.

With most breeds or types we know broadly why and what our ancestors were trying to create but we will never know all the details. We know for certain even less about the lurcher than some other types for the simple reason that so few written or visual records featuring them exist from the past. Considering the purposes for which most lurcher owners used their dogs and the penalties should they have been caught, small wonder they were so reticent.

— 2 —
The Lurcher Today

Unlike the running dog of 50 years ago when, before the most recent agricultural revolution, a farmer reckoned a ton of barley to the acre to be a fairish crop, the lurcher of today is seldom required to fill his traditional role of driving a hare into a gate net or a rabbit into a longnet. Most of the hedgerows alongside which we used to put down our nets have gone as have the gateways and the gate nets with them. As a result of so-called progress a different type of dog has emerged to operate in present day conditions. Perhaps I should say types of dog rather than type for it has become very much a matter of 'horses for courses' or 'hounds for grounds'.

THE LAMPING DOG

Just as once the main function of a lurcher was to manoeuvre the game into a net one might justifiably come to the conclusion that today it is lamping by night. There are other uses for such a dog but there can be little doubt that, although understandably no official statistics on the matter exist, the majority of quarry is taken in this way. For this sort of work it is of the greatest importance that the dog should be possessed of, above all, vast reserves of stamina. This is the main consideration but it should also have enough sense to be able to work out the way to connect with its target before it gets to ground. Sense of smell is not important and in fact the less that the dog is endowed in this respect the better. Neither is any sort of abnormal speed required in such a dog.

A Lurcher speeding at full stretch about to take the quarry.

THE FERRETING DOG

The ferreter on the other hand will be looking for different talents in his ideal coney dog. What he wants is something which is agile and nippy, a dog with colossal acceleration, this being more important than stamina and the ability to keep on making run after run like the lamping dog. His lurcher will also need to have a good nose and to be readily trainable to keep still wherever it is stationed although always ready to explode into instant action whenever necessary.

THE FOXING DOG

Except in some of the wilder parts of the United Kingdom, where foxhounds were either unable to operate, or at best could only do so on a restricted basis, the old time lurcher was rarely called upon to tackle a fox. The situation today is a very different one. With motorways and highspeed railways all over the place, and the ever increasing amount of land taken up by urban sprawl and industrial development, there is less and less land available over which to hunt. The activities of hunt saboteurs and the growing economic importance of shoots have also made things more and more difficult for the organisers of fox hunting and many farmers and landowners no longer wish to see foxhounds on their land.

With some packs the number of foxes killed is so abysmally low that one could be excused for thinking that the hounds are out merely for the purpose of being exercised, as are the horses. Many hunt followers go out only for the ride and with no thought of keeping down the number of foxes,

Max a Bull Terrier/Greyhound cross owned by Doug Sanders of Cumbria, a powerhouse of a dog.

which meanwhile continue to proliferate, particularly in the urban surroundings to which they are rapidly adapting themselves and where the living is easy. Whilst this no doubt suits the urban fox fancier and the maker of television wild life features very well it is not good news for the poultry and sheep farmer.

Although on the face of things the followers of organised fox hunting and the animal rights activists are poles apart the main intention of the majority of people in both camps is one and the same, to preserve foxes at all costs. No wonder the poultry farmer turns to the lurcherman for assistance as does the more general farmer who is fed up with the hunt riding over his young corn and disturbing his in-lamb ewes. From these strictures I completely exonerate the footpacks of the Lakeland Fells who maintain a completely sane and balanced view about the matter. In most of the other countries where hunt followers are mounted I should think that it would be no exaggeration to say that many more foxes are destroyed by means of running dogs and terriers than as a result of formal foxhunting.

Quite a number of rabbiting lurchers are not at all bad on fox although, should one intend to concentrate on specialised vermin destruction of this nature, probably something larger and more powerful is needed. Indeed this is one of the instances when I would prefer to use a longdog rather than a lurcher. Not that I have any intention of denigrating the foxing lurcher but this is the sort of work where your dog must be able to settle the matter in as swift and efficacious a manner as is possible; there must be no question of any sort of a fight ensuing. The end must be sudden and final.

THE HARE DOG

All sorts of claims may be heard on the part of lurcher owners, these being at their loudest in the beer tents at shows, but there can be little doubt that the main quarry of the lurcher of today is no longer the hare, as it was in times gone by, but the humble rabbit. In fact, since the use of nets combined with lurchers has suffered if not a demise at least a considerable decline, it can be safely said that the great majority of hares coursed by dogs are taken by longdogs as distinct from lurchers.

THE RIGHT DOG

One fact if no other emerges when one considers lurchers in the light of present day conditions and it is that herding ability is by no means as necessary as it used to be. For today's work a much more specialised kind of animal is needed, and whilst it is indeed a joy to own and work with an all round and easily trainable dog there is a very definite trend towards

Stephen Robinson's Bedlington/Whippet in hot pursuit.

the specialist. Thus for daytime rabbiting the smaller more agile dog with spectacular initial take off speed is preferred, whilst a dog with a good deal more stamina but with less nose is the one for lamping, a larger and more powerful dog being favoured for taking foxes. Rather different types of lurcher from the past have, therefore, already evolved and, as I see it, are still evolving. Fortunately for us the very nature of the lurcher enables us to achieve the results which we seek with far less difficulty than would be the case with dogs of pure blood, for the mixture of breeds in the lurcher need by no means be kept constant.

Today's lurcher will probably be, first and foremost, a rabbiting dog and probably for most people an all-round lurcher means an all-round coney dog. Can one find this in a single dog? If one is prepared to put up with a certain amount of scenting ability in a lamping dog perhaps one can for it is quite possible to find both initial take off speed and stamina in the same animal.

THE SHOW DOG

Another way in which the lurcher of today differs from the dog of the past is solely due to those modern phenomena, the lurcher show and the obedience trial. Fifty years ago such events were unknown and if anyone had suggested holding such a thing it is very likely that he would have been the subject of some very funny looks, for if anyone had a lurcher the chances were that he would tend to keep the fact fairly quiet. Circumstances alter though and today's lurcherman reflects the general attitudes and conventions of the time in which we live. In the past the owner of such a dog would in all probability have kept it solely to poach game but today the situation is somewhat different and along with the change of emphasis regarding the main quarry from the hare to the rabbit the present day lurcher owner is more likely to be some sort of pest controller than anything else, whether or not he is paid for his services.

Such a person has no qualms about anyone else knowing all about his dog and is willing, and in many cases eager, to parade its many virtues

Richard Gregory with Bracken, winner of The Cock 'O' The North Championship, at Wolsingham Show, Co. Durham, 1990.

before the public, one aspect of this increased openness being the lurcher show. The lurcher show which started off as a bit of fun on a Sunday afternoon, while at the same time doing a bit of good for one's favourite charity, has now in many instances become a matter of deadly seriousness to some lurcher owners. Their dogs have but one purpose in life and that is to win rosettes at shows. The entrants are prinked up and prettified for each event and deadly postmortems worthy perhaps of something more akin to Cruft's, are to be heard concerning the results both during and after such competitions. Taking an unbiased view of the lurcher shows which one attends, it could be fairly safely said that many of the classes are won not by lurchers but by longdogs particularly those carrying a good deal of Deerhound blood. I can think of at least one pure bred Deerhound which has won a supreme championship. The reason for this is that dogs of this type please the eye and a show is a beauty contest when all is said and done.

LURCHERS IN PRINT

Further evidence of the change in attitude can be seen in the number of books which are available today on the subject of lurchers when previously information concerning them was exceedingly sparse. You will find fleeting references to such dogs in books of the Victorian era but perhaps the first person to write about them in any detail was Brian Vesey-Fitzgerald, one time editor of the Field and a lifelong companion of gypsies and travelling people generally. He contributed a short article about lurchers in *The Book Of The Dog* which was published in 1948 and again mentioned them in his classic, *It's My Delight*, which came out about the same time. Interestingly in one of these volumes he says that the lurcher is based on a cross between Greyhound and collie and in the other he describes it as a Greyhound/Bedlington Terrier mixture.

COLOUR

Still comparing then with now, there seems to be a good deal less strong feeling these days in respect of colour. Time was when no one wanted to know anything about any sort of lurcher, no matter how good a dog it happened to be, should its coat be anything other than brindle or black, some favouring one and some the other. Nowadays there are those who will only have a merle coloured dog, despite the well known drawbacks connected with breeding from dogs with this type of marking. One even sees gay pied and white dogs these days. This can only indicate the growing respectability of most, if not all, lurchers and their owners. No poacher would want to own a dog that stood out at night as clearly as a white or would identify him as easily as a distinctively marked merle.

HOW VERSATILE?

Quite recently I was admiring a very fine Norfolk type lurcher in a pub, which I sometimes frequent, when I suddenly realised that its owner was completely blind. Yes, that's right, outlandish as it would have seemed to be at one time, his lurcher was his guide dog. Not surprisingly he confirmed that it had never been entered to any sort of quarry, but he mentioned that its ownership had involved him in some very interesting conversations. This must prove more than anything else the complete versatility of the lurcher in its modern form.

— 3 —
Lurchers Around the World

When one starts to think about lurchers in foreign lands, one immediately becomes aware of just how few of them there are in places outside the British Isles. My travels have taken me over a fairly large proportion of the world's surface; I still keep active contact with places in Africa and Australia and I can confirm that there are precious few lurchers in most of the places with which I am acquainted. Longdogs, yes; there are fair numbers of those about in the shape of kangaroo hounds down under, Salukis in some of the Arab states and cold-blood Greyhounds and their ilk in the States, but lurchers as we recognise them over here, precious few.

Some of the byblows of the longdogs which I have mentioned, undoubtedly exist in the places where these are found but here I feel that we must not forget that the breeding of a proper lurcher is a planned affair, a deliberate cross. In any case the results of indiscriminate couplings with pye-dogs can be nothing more than yet more pye-dogs and so that is the end of that line of breeding before it has even commenced. One would expect more 'roo hound crossings with cattle dogs in the antipodes but this does not seem to happen; I suppose the very marked differences in size may have something to do with this. Many kangaroo hounds, which incidentally tackle things like wild pig as well, scale up to nearly a hundredweight and stand up to a metre in height.

AUSTRALIA

But as they say, where there's a will there's a way and the locally famous Red Dog which unaccompanied travelled the highways of Western Australia by bus was almost certainly a result of one such unplanned union. One thing is fairly certain about him, that his dam was a cattle dog. Judging by the dog's conformation there must have been something of the longdog in his make up as well. For anyone who is interested in this somewhat unusual creature there are not only a few photographs of him around in the places to which his spectacular journeys were wont to take him but also there is a statue erected to his memory just near the bus stop outside Karratha which was his favourite bus boarding place. For Red Dog's fame is based on just that, his remarkable ability to travel about the countryside never using any other means of doing so than public transport. From his base, which seems to have been somewhere in the vicinity of Karratha, he travelled to out of the way spots like Tom Price and Carnarvon and Paraburdoo, on at least two occasions making the journey to the big city, Perth itself, involving a round trip of some 2,500 miles. He so captured the public imagination that most of the young unmarried chaps in the north-west subscribed a monthly sum towards his upkeep, paying not only the cost of his rations but also for things like inoculations, finally raising a statue by public subscription to his everlasting memory. Not the result of deliberate breeding, not a true lurcher, not a hunting dog but a travelling dog and something like a lurcher, which is perhaps more than can be said about some of the results of more meticulously planned liaisons.

AFRICA

So much for Australia. Africa also had its longdogs and I have described in *The Working Longdog* how I came by a Wolfhound, which was perhaps one of Graham's original line. Miles Fletcher, my neighbour at Ngobit, as befitted a Tasmanian, had a kangaroo hound and a close acquaintance, Michael Sugden had a Greyhound. The only lurchers which were bred from any of these, if lurchers they could have been said to be, were those which I bred myself by crossing Wolfhound with Alsatian. I have always averred that lurchers they were, being hybrids between sighthounds and pastoral breed but I do not feel so strongly about the matter as to take serious issue with anyone who might have differing views on the subject, the point which I am making is simply that there were very few lurchers about in Africa during my days there. There must be still less of them now that a total hunting ban exists in so many African states.

EUROPE AND U.S.A.

Not having struck much paydirt in my own recollections of the existence, or rather non-existence of lurchers overseas, I consulted well known Midlands lurcher breeder, David Hancock, on the matter. I was aware that David fairly regularly exports lurchers but to where? He informs me that by far the greater number go to the United States with a few to Germany and even fewer to Greece and the island of Rhodes. Well, it takes a Yank to know a good thing, that's for sure, and if you have read the articles written by Mrs Teddy Moritz concerning her exploits with a couple of lurchers and a few assorted terriers and Dachshunds in her home state of New Jersey, you will realise that her dogs, bred by David Hancock incidentally, are used to some purpose in pursuit of coon and coyote, woodchuck and fox as well as other assorted transatlantic varmintry.

I am told that the lurchers which go to Germany are very well regarded for their scenting abilities being used in the well organised trailing tests which they hold there, the object of the competition being that each dog shall be required to follow a cold drag of deer's blood which has been laid 24 hours previously. Those which go to Greece are used for hunting such hares as are to be found there, the running grounds consisting of stone walled, boulder strewn olive groves.

This all goes to show the general versatility of the lurcher but nevertheless, the true lurcher is a dog which was originally developed for hunting the small to medium sized enclosures of the countryside of Old England, a countryside the field boundaries of which were delineated by well layered hedgerows and at whose entrances were well hung gates, a countryside where a dog would work a hare to a gate net or rabbits to a long net, sometimes varying these activities by picking up the odd pheasant from hedgerow and partridge from stubble. The fact that any of them can also have been put to useful work overseas speaks volumes as to their worth as sporting dogs.

What of the Ibizan and Pharoah Hounds? True, they are used all over the western Mediterranean region but are they lurchers? Not within the definition of a lurcher as a cross bred dog I would be inclined to think.

— 4 —
Lurcher Crosses

Sheepdog Crosses

In its original form the sheepdog was one of the archetypal breeds of working dog but, alas, with the exception of the Border Collie this is no longer strictly true. Sadly most breeds of pastoral dog no longer perform what should be their proper function of herding or guarding sheep. Many of them are bred for show or as pets, having very little or no working instinct; even amongst Border Collies some are now being bred with the primary objective of winning prizes in such contrived events as sheep dog trials and obedience tests. Whilst events of this nature started as a bit of Sunday afternoon fun, as is the way with so many things, they have become ends in themselves and highly competitive. This has led in turn to the breeding of a certain type of dog that excels at these competitions rather than being an all round worker.

However, working types of sheepdog are still to be found and some of these are quite satisfactory for crossing with Greyhounds and Whippets in order to produce lurchers, some of which can be useful sorts. The collies which I would regard as being suitable in this respect are those which come from good, steady, well-founded working strains, which above all possess steadiness and a complete absence of any form of excitability. Such dogs are not as common as some might have us think.

THE DIFFERENT TYPES OF SHEEPDOG

Before proceeding any further we may as well dismiss from our minds any considerations of breeding lurchers by using any of the continental breeds

A Border Collie herding sheep.

of sheepdog such as the Italian Maremma, the Hungarian Komondor and Kuvasz, the Carpathian Sheepdog of Romania and such dogs as the Cao Serra da Estrela of Portugal. Fine looking creatures as they are, although coming within the nomenclature of sheepdogs, their mission in life when employed in a working capacity is to guard their flocks against the depredations of such predators as wolves and they would never be used in a herding capacity.

Having narrowed the field to some extent we are now in a position to consider what remains, consisting as it does of our native breeds, the Border Collie, the Bearded Collie, the Rough Collie and the Old English Sheepdog with the addition of a comparatively late arrival on the scene, the Australian Cattle Dog. I suppose that I might have included the German Shepherd but, after a certain amount of consideration I have included it under Guard Dogs, which these days it has to all intents and purposes become.

THE ROUGH COLLIE

Of these dogs let us first take a slightly closer look at the Rough Collie, the Scotch Collie as it used to be called in the days of my youth. It is conceivable that at some time in the dim and distant past it may have been

18

quite a useful working sheepdog. Indeed this must have been the case for otherwise, as a breed it would probably not have survived. This was one of the first of the breeds to suffer at the hands of the showring fraternity. A dog of this breed was placed first at the earliest dog show which catered for sheepdogs in 1860. The Rough Collie continued to enjoy a very great degree of popularity in dog shows from that date until the end of the nineteenth century, during this period achieving the distinction of becoming one of the two highest priced breeds in this country. The usual cost of distinction in the showring swiftly followed and such dogs became complete non starters as far as working livestock was concerned. It has been alleged that in order to produce the long, narrow, dolichocephalic heads which were so sought after by the fancy, a good measure of Borzoi blood was brought in. If one were to be narrowly dogmatic it might be said that this produced some kind of lurcher, for here was a breed of longdog being crossed with a sheepdog. This just goes to prove that putting any sort of longdog to any sort of sheepdog does not automatically produce the sort of hunting animal that anyone might want.

Whoever first hit upon, what must have seemed to him at the time to be a bright idea, no doubt congratulated himself upon having improved the dog's appearance no end. In the process the working abilities of the breed were ruined, but I do not suppose this ever troubled his conscience. From the point of view of using one of these dogs for working sheep the idea is best forgotten, just as should be any thought of breeding lurchers from them.

THE OLD ENGLISH SHEEPDOG

The Old English Sheepdog has been with us for a very long time. It is depicted in drawings and paintings by Van Eyck and Durer as long ago as the fifteenth century. In later works by Gainsborough and Bewick it is shown even more graphically and it is interesting to note that these dogs are not docked and do not carry anything like as much hair about their legs, rather resembling a larger version of today's Bearded Collie. This backs up the description by a noted authority on the breed that in the mid nineteenth century the coat was considerably shorter, as was the hair on top of the head, with no sign of shagginess and with a 'Greyhound' type of face. Another fancier of the time described the dogs as being 'formed after the model of a strong, low Greyhound', which sounds remarkably like a description of the socalled Smithfield.

It seems the breed went out of fashion for a time and dogs shown at the Birmingham event of 1873 probably mark the time of its comeback. One of the early recreators of the breed was R.J. Lloyd Price of Rhiwlas in Wales, but this should not be taken as an indication that the breed was Welsh in origin for it is on record that Lloyd Price obtained his foundation stock from Sussex. This would seem to point to some connection with the Sussex Bobtail, one of the old breeds of herding dog which is now said to be extinct.

There must have been quite a number of dogs about in the early part of this century which were of this type. As a boy in Lincolnshire in the 1920s I well remember there being sheepdogs which were habitually referred to as Old Lincolnshire Bobtails. In fact we had a shepherd, a man named Adamson, who worked one of these to sheep and it was by no means an uncommon sort of dog in the neighbourhood; that would be about 1926. In 1971 my wife was working on the census and at Graveney in North Kent, whilst engaged in enumerating one particular household, she spotted a dog which so took her fancy that she insisted on my going and looking at it. Its owner told me that it was one of the Old Norfolk Turkey Hounds which at one time had been used to herd the turkeys from the Eastern Counties to Smithfield; yes, that name again. I would have placed the animal as one of the Old Lincolnshire Bobtails in probably much the same way as a native of the Sussex downlands would have recognised it as one of the Old Sussex Bobtails. Younger persons with less experience of the ways of sheep and shepherds of yesteryear but a more up to date acquaintance with Cruft's would have almost certainly marked it down as a Bearded Collie.

Was something of this nature the foundation stock which Lloyd Price obtained from Sussex? It is my belief that it probably was. From general appearance alone there would not seem to be much doubt that the Old English and the Bearded have some sort of common origin and that not very far back in time.

As with the Rough Collie this is not a breed suitable for work today, or for crossing to produce a satisfactory lurcher.

THE BEARDED COLLIE

In recent years some collie lurcher enthusiasts have been promoting the Bearded Collie as the ideal to cross with a Greyhound. I am not convinced as to their suitability since most are now of show stock and of dubious working ability. Even if we can find one from working stock I am not sure that they are ideal from either the point of view of temperament or coat.

Information regarding the origins of the Bearded Collie is incomplete as well as bizarre. The story is that the founding stock were brought to Scotland by some Polish seafarer who bartered his wonder dogs for some, one assumes, equally spectacular sheep. This account is fairly well known if not universally believed. It is a story which seems to have gained to some extent in the telling. In some of the current versions even the name of he who brought the dogs is known; it is Grabski, we are told. All this is alleged to have occurred in the reign of James I of England (James VI of Scotland), a monarch whose origins are also a little in doubt. Although undoubtedly

Bearded Collie/Greyhound.

of ancient origin the Bearded Collie seems to have gone into eclipse for in 1945 it was described by one authority as being extremely rare and to be found on only a few farms in Peebles-shire although, had he taken the trouble to continue his enquiries in some of the remoter parts of places like Lincolnshire and Sussex, I dare say he might have found another odd one or two.

Whatever truth may be attached to the account of the importation of the Bearded Collie from Poland it is my own opinion that the Old English and the Bearded had one and the same origin, in common with the various other regional British breeds of similar sort, not leaving out the legendary Smithfield. By a process of natural selection the larger dogs, such as the Old English, were used for cattle droving, the smaller ones, like the Bearded, being employed for herding sheep. Why did these two breeds go into disuse? It would seem likely that the Old English and similar varieties first went into decline when the introduction of railways ended the old practice of herding the animals to market. The changing farming scene resulted in the need for a biddable and less robust dog to herd the sheep and cattle around the farm, hence the rise in popularity of the Border Collie.

The day that I see either a Bearded Collie or an Old English Sheepdog taking part in sheepdog trials, let alone winning at them, is the day that I might just consider using one or the other of these dogs for lurcher breeding. Even then I would think twice about the matter for no matter how intelligent and biddable the dog, I still would not much fancy owning a dog which was frequently having to be cut adrift from brambles and thorns, or which resembled something like the Abominable Snowman in wintery weather. Those who are the most vocal in their praises for Bearded Collies and their lurcher crosses parade as a virtue the fact that these dogs are sometimes difficult to lead train. Whether or not this is so, a dog which will not be trained to the lead is of no use to me nor, I should think, to any other sensible person.

A Bearded Collie from known working stock is a possible cross, but perhaps one better suited to the more experienced lurcher owner. The first timer might find some of them difficult to train and work.

THE BORDER COLLIE

The Border Collie has certain characteristics which make it today a very popular choice for crossing with a Greyhound to create a lurcher. The Border Collie is still predominately a working dog and is plentiful in all

A David Hancock three-quarter bred merle Border Collie/Greyhound cross.

parts of the country so it is not too difficult to find a suitable brood bitch or stud dog. It is not only easy to train and biddable but many of its abilities, such as herding, are a sublimated form of hunting making it an ideal choice for the other half of the cross. For those wanting good looks as much as hunting ability the three-quarter breed will fulfil this requirement and then of course the merle colouring found in certain crosses is very distinctive and popular these days. The Border Collie has stamina, is reasonably fast and is strongly built, so when crossed it complements the Greyhound and with luck one ends up with a good looking animal with a good turn of speed, virtually indestructible, jaws capable of killing a fox, biddable and the stamina to run all night.

The perfect dog has yet to be born, of course, and in reality one always has to work with and know a dog's strengths and weaknesses. With any coin there are always two sides and while in some combinations the Border Collie might be the ideal cross for today's lurcher some most definitely are not.

There are, of course, Border Collies which never take part in trials, but are well able to carry out any sort of herding functions which are required of them. There are also Border Collies which are unlikely to be much good for anything, some being poor in intelligence, others conformation, and some both.

Border Collies have been almost universally used for herding sheep in this country for most of this century. When I was very young, one used to see dogs like this around which were referred to as Welsh Sheepdogs and I remember one dog in particular which people said was a Cumberland

A half-bred Border Collie/Greyhound.

To my mind the Border Collie Lurcher is very much a one man dog for the one dog man. David Crow with his Collie/Greyhound, Bess.

Sheepdog. This one had come from a farm on Lord Lonsdale's estate at Lowther. It was a very useful animal indeed. A smallish dog, I remember it as always seeming to work close to the ground and being rather a quiet animal, utterly unlike some of the Bobtails which had been around previously.

Border Collies from good working strains are, on the whole, excellent dogs but occasionally they can prove to be nervy and highly strung. When breeding collie based lurchers one must be exceedingly careful about the temperaments of the foundation animals. If you are buying rather than breeding a lurcher, which is a Border Collie cross, be on the lookout for undesirable traits of this nature in both the pup and its bloodline. Of all the lurchers which have come my way more animals of this breeding have exhibited these undesirable characteristics than lurchers of other breed crosses.

Another possible characteristic for which you should be on the look out, should your fancy be for a Border Collie bred lurcher, is an inbuilt proneness to carry any lesson, once learned, rather to excess. This, I am sure, is all part of the overpowering desire of such dogs to please. Some will herd to excess, any mortal thing will do, from cattle to sheep to poultry to small children. Others, having been trained to retrieve some object or other, such as a ball, will continue to do this to the point of making a nuisance of themselves. Whatever your feelings may be concerning this frenzied retrieving which in itself, although tiresome, is relatively harmless, any propensity towards carrying their herding instincts too far should be severely curbed for taken to its ultimate stage it can result in stock worrying.

To my mind the Border Collie lurcher is very much a one man dog for the one dog man. Many of them are of a jealous disposition which is not always immediately obvious and I would never kennel a dog of this kind together with another dog, particularly one of a smaller sort. A very good friend of mine, who spares no effort or expense as far as his dogs are concerned, purchased a Border Collie bred lurcher from a very highly recommended source and paid a fairly large sum for what he fancied. The dog which had never exhibited any signs of viciousness, as far as anyone was aware, suddenly turned on a terrier with which it had been kennelled for the previous seven years and bit its head clean off. From that moment it showed such signs of hostility towards all this chap's other dogs, both male and female, that he had no compunction in having it put down.

Assuming that you have decided that a collie lurcher is the only dog for you, where do you go from here? Is it to be a half bred or a three-quarter bred (by three-quarter bred I refer to a dog which is three-quarters Greyhound)? It all depends what you want it for, of course, but I can only give advice based upon my own and others' experience. I have yet to meet a man who has acquired a half bred dog and been entirely satisfied with it, the main reason being that most of them are considerably lacking in speed. I would, therefore, advise anyone interested in this sort of lurcher to go in for a three-quarter bred. These do not seem to be less intelligent than the half bred to any marked degree.

Not a great deal is heard about the Whippet/collie cross these days but, for a rabbiting dog, one of these can be very useful. As with the larger Greyhound cross the three-quarter bred is usually superior to the straight cross but, since not quite so much is being demanded of it, some of the half breds of the lighter sort can be quite satisfactory. I have always thought that the Whippet cross has the edge on the larger Greyhound crosses as far as intelligence goes. No more should be expected from such a dog than an ability to catch rabbits and rats; it is just not big enough to be expected to take on anything much larger, lacking the stamina to deal with a hare and the weight to tackle a fox. Nevertheless, if I were keen to have a collie lurcher for rabbiting only, this is certainly a cross which I should consider.

OTHER SIGHTHOUND CROSSES

Collie crosses with any sort of sighthound blood other than Greyhound or Whippet are seldom encountered, and I can only say that those which I have met have left no lasting impression on me. Someone introduced some Border Collie blood into my own line of Deerhound hybrids and the results were not spectacular, the offspring being not dissimilar from their Deerhound parent. A Borzoi/Border Collie cross which I encountered had nothing that I could see to recommend it, although the Border Collie part of the breeding was one of the best that I know. My advice to anyone contemplating the acquisition of a collie lurcher would be to stick to the three-quarter Greyhound cross. However, it is always well to bear in mind that although many animals of this blood will give every satisfaction and indeed in some cases, a good deal more, they are not all wonder dogs and they all need to be thoroughly trained in just the same way as any other dog.

THE AUSTRALIAN CATTLE DOG

A recent introduction to the British lurcher scene is the Australian Cattle Dog. There are not many of these about but I know of two which are in the hands of experienced lurchermen in the South of England. Like many other canines the origins of the cattle dog from down under are shrouded in a certain amount of mystery. It would certainly appear that the wild dog of Australia, the dingo, has some place in the mixture having in early days in the colony been crossed with collies imported from Britain to produce the first versions of the Australian Cattle Dog, also known as the Heeler. This blood was later ameliorated with that of the Dalmatian, an unlikely choice one might have thought, until one remembers the old association of the spotted dogs with horses. Dalmatians are fairly closely related to the English Pointer and trained as a setting dog will still give a good account of themselves on the shooting field, but they really made their mark in the days of the Regency when it was almost de rigeur to have one of these dogs trotting beneath the rear axle of one's perch phaeton. This alone is indicative of the stamina of such a dog.

Since herding in the outback is carried out on horseback the introduction of Dalmatian blood would seem to have been a sensible one and the result must almost certainly have proved to be satisfactory for the breed was fixed at this point. It is early days as yet, certainly too early to judge what may be the ultimate result of the cross between Greyhound and Australian cattle dog. There is nothing static about the world of lurchers and any innovation which works successfully is to be welcomed; this cross may prove to be a most interesting addition.

SHEEPDOGS IN GENERAL

To revert to the subject of sheepdogs in general I can say without the least hesitation that some I have encountered were superb working dogs, the very best imaginable, but others were the very worst villains, and if they are bad, they are very, very bad. Quite a few of those of working stock which I have seen on outlying farms have been downright vicious and whatever their working qualities might have been, were not the sort of dogs which would be acceptable in more sophisticated surroundings. Their viciousness usually takes the form of sly biting so that whilst your attention is engaged by something else, perhaps the farmer whom you have visited on a matter of business, they will slink up behind and take a good nip at your calf. Cross one of these brutes with a Greyhound of similar temperament and you are really in trouble. Sheep worrying on the part of such dogs is not altogether unknown.

So should your fancy be for a collie lurcher, just make sure firstly that the sheepdog side of the family is from a good working strain and secondly that such working strain is sound beyond a doubt as regards temperament. Border Collies, although of undoubted pedigree, are often cheaply available for a variety of reasons. To cross one of these with any old Greyhound, which is to be had for nothing, will produce a lurcher sure enough but this is by no means an unfailing recipe for success. As with many things in life you tend to get what you pay for.

CONCLUSION

If you are looking specifically for a lamping lurcher then the Border Collie/Greyhound three-quarter bred is the cross I suggest you look at. If you are thinking about a Bearded Collie/Greyhound cross then again look for a three-quarter bred, but give the matter some consideration before taking the plunge and buying a dog of this breeding. If you are interested in winning rosettes at shows this is not the cross for you.

The collie cross is likely to be the most biddable of all the crosses and, therefore, easy to train. But it can be heavily built, slow and have what the average lurcher man would consider to be temperament problems. At one end of the scale you have the dog that is a delightful companion and excellent lamping dog and at the other a favoured tool of destruction of those who go after some highly illegal forms of quarry.

Terrier Crosses

Almost as popular today as the Border Collie cross lurcher is the Bedlington Terrier/Whippet or Greyhound cross. This is a particularly popular choice with the rabbiting and ferreting man.

THE BEDLINGTON

The Bedlington/Whippet cross is rightly popular for the record of such dogs is an impressive one. On rabbit and small vermin they are second to none always assuming, of course, that the right sort of blood is present on both sides of the breeding. It is fairly easy to find a Whippet which, given the right sort of encouragement and environment, will become a resourceful hunter. The purebred Whippet takes a lot of beating as a pot filler for, let's face it, this has been the role of the breed for centuries. It has always been the dog of the rural independent, the man who bowed the knee to no one and who, under the right sort of circumstances, never suffered from the indignity of having an empty stewpot. It has also for many years been the dog of the heavy industrial worker, the dog which, living indoors as a household pet, was still capable of going out and providing next Sunday's dinner. Such dogs were bred and reared not for their beauty and conformation but largely for their working ability, which had been further tried in the fire of local Whippet racing contests.

Like the Greyhound, Whippets tend roughly to fall into the categories of track dogs and coursing dogs but, again like the Greyhound, the difference between the two types tends to be rather blurred and many a good track dog is able to give a good account of itself in the field and vice versa. When the Whippet blood is to be ameliorated with that of a terrier of the right sort, the differing virtues of the two types of Whippet become less important. Nevertheless, I would always endeavour to breed from a strain of Whippet which has stood the test of the coursing field.

Obtaining a suitable Bedlington, however, presents us with rather more

A Bedlington/Whippet retrieves a rabbit live to hand.

in the way of difficulties than obtaining the right sort of Whippet for this is where the hand of the show breeder begins to appear. I think there can be little doubt that scarcely any breed of dog exists which has not suffered from the lengths to which the dog showing fraternity will go in order to make their dogs more acceptable in the judge's eye. This is the reason for having to exercise a very great deal of care in the selection of Bedlington blood in the breeding of small lurchers.

The Bedlington Terrier of 50 years ago was a totally different animal from the show specimens which one may see on a visit to Cruft's on a February day. Not only was the conformation of the terrier completely dissimilar but its temperament was entirely at odds with the show Bedlingtons of today. The show people in order to fix the type they desired had to go in for line breeding and this is where things started to go wrong for line breeding is but another way of describing inbreeding. Cynics have been heard to comment that the difference between line breeding and inbreeding is that line breeding is when the result is satisfactory and

George Newcombes' Bedlington stud dog, Blue.

inbreeding is when matters take a less than desirable turn. The whole point about the process is that it has a disturbing way of fixing not only desired characteristics but also some highly unacceptable ones as well, and this is what seems to have occurred in the show Bedlington for the very simple reason that these dogs were line bred with looks rather than working ability as the goal. To add insult to injury bad breeding has led to the Bedlington having a very poor quality fluffy curly coat. The result has been to transform the Bedlington Terrier into something closer in type to the miniature poodle than anything else in the canine world.

This takes the Bedlington Terrier of today a very long way indeed from the dog of former times, the one whose blood was used from time to time to improve that of the Fell Terrier whenever the owners believed that their dogs were beginning to lack a bit of fire. There are, however, a few conscientious and committed breeders who have striven to keep the old type of Bedlington going. The foremost of these must be George Newcombe of Rillington near Malton and the late Mrs Williamson with her Gutchcommon strain. Each of them endeavoured to maintain the right type of Bedlington, although interestingly enough they each sought to achieve the result by a different means. Newcombe achieved what he considered to be the perfect animal by outcrossing to other terrier blood. There can be no doubt whatsoever that George Newcombe's Bedlingtons are very good indeed.

Mrs Williamson on the other hand refused to bring in any outside blood but bred by careful selection within the breed from those Bedlingtons which she considered to be the right sort and which were available to her. What is certain, whatever the individual merits of either method, is that in both cases the results were extremely satisfactory, providing a gutsy, sensible sort of terrier, a working terrier one might recommend without any qualms.

If you are looking for a Bedlington Terrier I would suggest you look for one which features either of these lines heavily in its pedigree. But the subject of this book is not the Bedlington Terrier, upon which there are others far better qualified than I to comment. If you should wish to read more on this subject I suggest you buy yourself a copy of John Glover's excellent book *The Working Bedlington* (1990, Dickson Price). In this context I have to say that I would go for the Gutchcommon blood every time and for one very good reason. Dogs of this strain and those derived from it have been bred over a considerable period, if not exactly to a particular line, then to a particular type. We, as lurcher breeders, are out-crossing in just about the most comprehensive way possible. Therefore, the fixed type is the one to go for. Excellent as the Newcombe Bedlingtons are, I would tend to avoid breeding lurchers from them for this very reason. The fairly regular introduction of extraneous blood, good as it is, must cause a certain amount of variation in the lurcher as the end product. On the whole, Bedlington/Whippet crosses are, like many first crosses, remark-ably level, but I have noticed that occasionally when the Rillington blood has been used, the crosses from such matings tend to be rather small, almost as though the union had been a direct Fell Terrier/Whippet one. However, dogs of this breeding, although frequently small, are very game and, for ferreting and bushing can hold their own with anything else.

This raises yet another matter, is the popular Bedlington/Whippet cross quite the right one for general all round use? Would not the Bedlington/Greyhound mixture be an even better one? Although something may be lost in the way of the Whippet intelligence, for very few Greyhounds can be quite the match for a Whippet in the way of canine I.Q., the larger size of even a 23 inch dog as against its Whippet cross counterpart, which will be doing well if it manages to make 18 inches in height, is something that merits consideration. The larger dog is faster, has more stamina and, whilst perhaps not quite so well supplied in the way of grey matter as the smaller dog, is nevertheless by no means short in this commodity.

This brings us to the other sorts of lurcher from terrier crosses and, although today the Bedlington lurcher is very much in evidence, other

A Bedlington/Whippet cross.

very successful crosses were popular in the past and I feel that it is about time that some adventurous breeders started to think about recreating some of these. First and foremost of these is the Airedale cross.

THE AIREDALE

This was a hybrid which was very much favoured in the North Lincolnshire of my youth. Not that there were many lurchers of any kind about there at that time. Just about all the land was in the hands of a few owners whose gamekeepers made abundantly sure of that. Ask anyone over the age of 75 in that neck of the woods, however, what sort of dogs the old General at Melton Ross used to breed and you will perhaps learn a bit about the Airedale/Greyhound cross.

Dispassionate examination of the true facts in the matter will reveal a few interesting points about the Airedale. I speak of course of the few strains which there are left of true working Airedales and there are a few, particularly in the foothills around Keighley and Bingley and Batley not to speak of some notable strains which exist in the United States. Alas, as with so many other breeds, the show fraternity have managed to ruin the working qualities of the breed with their boring and everlasting search after some strange form of conformity. Fortunately, progress in this direction has not been quite so brisk as it was with the Bedlington, the fate of which was being bewailed by no less a person than Brian Vesey-Fitzgerald away back in the 1940s, and the animals have therefore not attained the overaccentuated and frankly ridiculous show points of the Bedlington.

Bred as it originally was from a judicious blend of the Otterhound and the old fashioned black-and-tan sporting terriers, which were common in the West Riding at the time, the Airedale was bound to be a winner. It has never attracted much attention amongst working terrier owners for the very sound reason that it is too large to go to ground. It was not created for that purpose although its black-and-tan ancestor was more than capable in this department of sporting activity. The breed must have come into existence round about the middle of the nineteenth century for there are records of their having been exhibited at agricultural shows in Yorkshire in the 1860s when they were referred to as Broken Haired Terriers. It was about 1880 when they were given an official name, this being the Bingley Terrier. They immediately became exceedingly popular so that the name was thought to be a bit too restrictive. The name, 'Waterside Terrier' was then adopted for them. This did not last long either before the present name was officially given to the breed.

Each of the names given to them has been a fair description of the dog at the particular time when it received it. The terrier was first bred in the Bingley district of Airedale for use on the waterside of the River Aire against otters and any other kind of riverine quarry including rats. Since not many people were altogether aware of the the the whereabouts of Bingley, today still quite a small place although better known than it was on account of the Building Society which it shares with neighbouring Bradford, the nomenclature of Airedale came into being as the breed rapidly became better known. In its time the breed was remarkably popular and this popularity lasted from the late nineteenth century until the 1914–18 war when it gradually went into decline until it reached its present small numbers. Why did this happen? One supposes that it was something to do with changing tastes and a general increasing predisposition on the part of the dog owning public towards smaller animals with correspondingly smaller appetites and of a size more suited to the urban and suburban residences into which the population of this country has been moving with ever accelerating rapidity.

The Airedale's use as a sporting dog has likewise gone into a decline. This has been due to the seriously increasing pollution of watercourses which has taken place over the last 70 years. I have been absent from the banks of the River Aire for far too long but I would expect that it has been many a long day since an otter was seen there. This has not, however, been the case all over the world. In the United States there is a continuing use of Airedales against the larger types of vermin which they have there and they were reckoned in East Africa, when I lived there, to be a very handy sort of dog to use against dangerous big game. John Hunter told me that when he was engaged in his clearance of buffalo from the Ol Arabel Valley, it was Airedales which provided the backbone of his pack. Down near Machakos I came across Miss Irwin who had a small pack composed of these dogs; these not only provided a good hunting dog for using against the lion which abounded around there at the time but also were well known as about the best guard dogs in the district. This was at the time of Mau Mau when any sort of dog was very likely to be called upon to prove its abilities in this respect.

Indeed it was for police and combat work that the working members of the breed were chiefly used in both the First and Second World Wars both by British Forces and also by their German counterparts, who have always been in the forefront of those employing dogs for various purposes connected with their work. After the War they were used a good deal by both the railway and the docks police. They have thus proved themselves in actual working conditions alongside such breeds as the German Shepherd and the Doberman, signifying that there is no shortage of either intelligence or staunchness in their general makeup. In those which I have known their only fault seemed to be a predisposition to bite first and find out afterwards when confronted with a suspicious stranger. Not everyone might regard this as being a fault of course. Their scenting powers derived from their Otterhound ancestry are very pronounced and, in every way, this would seem to be a very suitable breed of dog to crossbreed with the Greyhound in order to produce a more than averagely useful sort of lurcher.

I would emphasise however that any Airedale used for lurcher breeding should be of proven working stock. Such does exist although it may take a good deal of finding these days when anyone who breeds purebred stock immediately seems to become dog show orientated. It is a very great pity that someone with the dedication which George Newcombe and Mrs Williamson brought to the breeding of the working Bedlington could not be found to revive the Airedale blood of old with perhaps a fresh dash of Otterhound and Lakeland blood to liven things up a bit. Were I 30 years younger I think this is one of the many things which I would do. As it is, why does not one of our sporting young men have a go?

A lurcher from this cross will probably come out at about 23 inches and around 40 lbs weight in working trim. Coats of such crosses tend to be fawn or tan just exhibiting signs of being broken. Such a dog should not be difficult to train and should enter to water and to jumping over obstacles without much difficulty.

A Bull Terrier/Greyhound. A cross with immense jaw power, at times a doubtful asset.

THE BULL TERRIER

Another terrier cross which turns up from time to time is that of the Bull
Terrier/Greyhound. Although on the face of it there might be certain

35

points to recommend it, this is not a cross which appeals to me a great deal. The trouble these days is to find the right sort of Bull Terrier and this applies just as much to the Staffordshire as to the English variety. I know that a good deal has been made of the superiority of the Staffordshire dogs over their rather more svelte cousins but speaking as I find, one of the gamest bitches that I ever encountered was of the English sort. One night she tackled a fully grown hyena, a beast scaling about 80 lbs and possessing a pair of jaws said to be more powerful than those of a lion. Without much of a fuss, she killed the brute single handed and then proceeded to drag the carcase in the direction of home. This was the only dog which I ever came across that was capable of such a feat single handed.

For this very reason I would be wary of such a cross with a Greyhound, for who wants a running dog with that sort of bite. Many of the other terrier crosses are bad enough in this respect but to deliberately introduce something with such a reputation for jaw power is, I think, asking for a good many mangled carcases. As well as this, Bull Terriers in my experience, do not have much in the way of scenting power. Whilst this is no drawback, indeed it is an asset in certain circumstances such as lamping, for the daytime hunter something with a bit more nose on it would be more attractive.

Should you decide that the Bull Terrier cross is the only one for you, then take heart for you are only carrying on the work of Lord Orford who many years ago introduced the Bulldog blood of the day into the Greyhound. This was in order to impart a bit of spirit into the hounds and is said to have had good effect, lasting until the present day some 200 years later. It is also reputed to be the reason why a good many Greyhounds have a brindle coat. So just bear in mind that a little Bull blood goes a Dickens of a long way.

THE IRISH TERRIER

In my young days there were quite a number of lurchers about which were the result of the Irish Terrier/longdog cross. It was usually a Whippet cross and these made exceedingly handy little rabbiting dogs. But then the Irishman has altered a very great deal since those days, when there were a fair few of them on farms and in country areas which were used for vermin control and at this they were able to give an exceedingly good account of themselves. The late Matthew Grass, who served his gamekeeping apprenticeship on the Duke of Westminster's Eaton Estate later to become Head Keeper on Sir Berkeley Sheffield's Normanby Park Estate, one of the finest preserves of game in the country at the time, always said that the best ratting dog that he had ever known was an Irish Terrier. Ratting, of course, much like everything else was a good deal different in those days, most of it being centred on corn ricks.

Ricks or stacks as we called them in the North of England provided snug winter quarters for the vermin with the added bonus of unlimited food. No wonder corn stacks proved to be such effective warrens; the vermin seemed to prefer wheat and oat stacks. I suppose the awns on the barley irritated them for one seldom encountered them in a barley stack. Depending on how hard pressed for cash the farmer happened to be, the stacks were threshed out earlier or later in the winter, the best time for this, of course, being during periods of frost or snow when it was not possible to get on to the land. When anyone was a bit strapped for cash the traction engine pulling its train of threshing machine, straw elevator and trusser, would be visiting his premises fairly soon after the harvest accompanied by winks and nods from his ever uncharitable neighbours with remarks of, 'There goes the Relieving Officer.'

The more affluent would often not thresh until well into spring, I suppose just to show all and sundry that their bank managers were not after them. This was the ideal situation for a good supply of healthy corn fed rats and there used to be some quite large bags. A wire mesh fence was erected around the rick prior to the start of the threshing operation and a useful sort of terrier was an absolute necessity. This was where the larger terriers such as the Irishman came into their own for they had sufficient stamina to keep on going when sport became fast and furious as the bottom of the stack was being reached. Most of the rodents would congregate there in order to make a mad dash at the last moment. On one such occasion, I was working on a corn stack and was wearing a boiler suit. A rat ran up my trouser leg and wound up under my armpit where I successfully squeezed it to death, fortunately not being bitten by it. I always made sure that I had something tight around my trouser bottoms after that when working amongst such hazards.

When combine harvesters arrived, such things as corn ricks and threshing machines rapidly became things of the past and there was not much in the way of work for the larger terriers. Their numbers were already somewhat in decline but this really seemed to spell the end of them. As far as the Irish Terrier is concerned this was a tragedy for it is a very old breed being mentioned in the Brehon Laws in third and fourth centuries. It was even claimed by some authorities that they were the descendants of bred down Wolfhounds. Although this does not seem altogether likely, the Irish Terrier probably has just as much, if not more, claim to relationship with the original Wolfhound than does the very artificial creation of the present day Irish Wolfhound, made up as it is of Deerhound and Mastiff with a bit of Great Dane thrown in for makeweight.

Irish Terriers go about 26 lbs in weight and 18 inches in height putting them sizewise about halfway between the Airedale and the Fox Terrier. This would seem to indicate that they might be an ideal dog to put on to a

Greyhound to produce some very useful lurchers since, their size and conformation is such that one does not need to go beyond the first cross, always a 'plus' factor in my estimation; they have plenty of drive, good noses and are active hunters. A lurcher bred from this first cross will probably come out at about 21 inches in height with a reddish broken coat. It would be nice to see a few such dogs about again.

THE KERRY BLUE AND THE WHEATEN

The Kerry Blue and the Wheaten Terrier differ from their countryman in one very important respect from the point of view of the lurcher breeder and this is that Irish Terriers have wiry coats as against the soft coats of the other two breeds. Perhaps it would be better if I were to say that they *should* have a wiry coat for it was always one of the troubles of the breed that they were occasionally born with soft silky coats. As far back as the early 1900s this was giving breeders a few problems. So far as I am able to ascertain, the troubles associated with breeding the silky coats was overcome about the time of the First World War and it would be very unusual to find this cropping up today.

A soft-coated Wheaten Terrier being paraded at Crufts.

THE JACK RUSSELL

Various breeds of terrier have been used to cross with longdogs either by design or occasionally by accident and the resultant offspring, as might be expected, are of varied type. A few years ago Jack Hargreaves produced something in the way of a minor sensation in one of the very entertaining programmes, which he used to put on TV, by showing something which he described as a Coney Dog. Several people whom I knew saw this show and asked me where they might obtain such a dog as that depicted, which was catching ferreted rabbits with never so much as a miss; every ball a coconut so to speak. As far as I was able to ascertain, the creature whose skills were so tellingly demonstrated, was some sort of a Jack Russell/Whippet cross.

As a result of these enquiries my interest was kindled although not to any marked degree. Later when I was passing through Canterbury I noticed just such a dog standing on the pavement outside a pub. I immediately went in to find out if anyone knew anything about the animal and was fortunate enough to be introduced to the owner and, as it turned out, breeder of the dog. Athirst for information, I questioned him about the breeding of the creature, how he came to decide on such a cross, what sort of worker it was, was it as good as the one which had been shown in the TV programme and so on. As soon as the poor chap had a chance to get a word into my spate of frantic questioning, he replied, 'Sorry, mate. That was just another pup that that damned Whippet left behind him. Maybe you saw him running about around here three or four years back. He left just about every bitch in the place in pup and mine was just another of them. To tell you the truth I've never thought of working it. Its mother didn't work either.'

Yet another blank had been drawn by your researcher.

THE TERRIER/GREYHOUND

The majority of lurchers emanating from terrier crosses seem to be the result of terrier/Whippet unions. Some of these are quite useful little rabbiting dogs but many of them are really too small to be much use other than for the sort of work where a terrier might be handier. As a good all round lurcher the terrier/Greyhound is hard to beat, given good working stock on both sides. Of these, the Bedlington cross is the most popular, resembling in many cases some sort of mini-Deerhound.

Why is there such a preference for dogs with this sort of appearance, whether it is the 26 to 28 inch Deerhound hybrid or its sometimes as small as 18 inch lookalike? I think that this must have some connection with the popular romantic conception of the lurcher. Of course, there are certain practical ways in which this kind of dog seems to be superior to the rest and I would say that these consist of stamina, speed and a weatherproof coat.

In the smaller Bedlington/Whippet cross these bonus points begin to rapidly fall away. They cannot do other than fall a bit short on both the stamina and speed of their larger counterparts and, as for the coat, this is often more inclined to being woolly than broken, thus being of doubtful worth.

CONCLUSION

If you are looking for an all round lurcher of terrier breeding you will find that there is a somewhat limited choice, since the main consideration must be that the terrier part of the make up should be from a good working strain, an elusive ideal these days when so many of the good old breeds of terrier, which did so well for us in the past, have been ruined by the demands of the show bench.

Providing that the terrier line carries the right blood, then I would say that the safest choice would be a three-quarter bred Bedlington/Greyhound. The Bedlington/Whippet has a considerable following but for every good one of these that I have encountered I would say that there are half a dozen which I should not want, many of them being just too small to be of much use; perhaps as a ferreting companion or for bushing, one of these might be suitable.

If the sort of appearance which will attract the eye of the average lurcher judge is what you are after, then the Bedlington cross with either Greyhound or Whippet will probably serve you the best.

Gundog Crosses

In those distant days before anyone had even thought about poison sprays, and artificial fertiliser was derisively referred to as 'bagmuck', there were very large quantities of both partridges and wild pheasants on all the large estates. These consisted of tenanted farms which were so often sold off and the estate broken up, or considerably diminished, in the postwar years.

In those days there was a larger number of gamekeepers, most of whom maintained at least two or three retrievers. Many of the tenant farmers also considered ownership of one of these dogs to be almost a sacred duty, particularly the favoured few who were invited for a day's shooting from time to time by the landlord, or the head keeper, depending upon which of these individuals considered himself to be in charge. In fact, on some estates farmers who kept any other sort of dog without good reason were not very popular with the powers that were.

Having recently been demobilised from the Army, I had been granted the tenancy of a small farm on the Normanby Estate. As soon as I was informed of this I went along to Wood House to break the news to my old friend and mentor, Matthew Grass, who was the head keeper there at the time. In the course of renewing our long standing friendship over a glass of the excellent Scotch with which he always seemed to be plentifully supplied, he enquired, 'Now that you have a farm you will need a dog. What sort are you going in for?'

There can have been no doubt that in his mind he expected a reply which would lead to a pleasant, and from his angle highly informed, discussion regarding the merits of Labrador as against Flatcoat, perhaps touching on Spaniels (in his opinion not a very good idea) or maybe Pointers or Setters (not for this sort of country). However, having been away from my native heath for nine or ten years by then and not choosing my words any too well, I replied: 'I was thinking of a Bedlington or something of that sort.'

He frostily regarded me with a slightly bemused expression, 'Surely you can't be serious,' he said. 'Here you are taking on all sorts of responsibilities now and I would have scarcely thought that you would have even considered anything of that sort.' I realised that I was regarded as being sadly in error and in the deathly hush which ensued my mind was churning round with all sorts of unlikely and unacceptable explanations concerning the suitability of such dogs for ratting and rabbiting and vermin control, when I became aware of Mrs Grass, a diplomat if ever there was one, saying: 'He's having you on, Matt. We all know that he's going to have one of Ralph Barrett's pups.'

I immediately and thankfully concurred, although to tell the truth what had been imparted was news to me for until then I did not even know that Lord St Oswald's head keeper had a bitch in whelp, let alone one with a saleable litter. However, there I was lumbered, as they say. Relations between Grass and myself returned to normal amidst a certain amount of head shaking and, 'They don't improve as they get older'. As soon as I left his house and had made my way to Burton Wood Top, I lost no time in heading for Appleby to see what might be available. To cut a long story short, after spending a happy hour or so talking to Barrett and looking at his dogs and his pheasant pens, I left there with a Labrador pup for which I had paid him the not exorbitant sum of £5, little enough to give for a dog with Banchory Bolo on both sides of the family. I never regretted the decision which had been forced upon me as a result of my thoughtless utterance and I merely relate the story in order to show the general attitude which existed in those days.

Given this preponderance of retrievers of various kinds which existed in rural areas in those days and the fact that both bitches and dogs were apt to wander rather more than they do in these traffic infested days, it was small wonder that the results of casual matings frequently carried retriever blood. There was also a good deal more official coursing going on then than there is today and consequently greater numbers of

Greyhounds about in country districts. What could be more natural than that retriever/Greyhound crosses should appear, either by design or accident, from time to time?

FIRST CROSSES

The first crosses from such a union almost always seem to be a bit inclined to heaviness, although this tends to be more pronounced when the retriever part of the equation is a Labrador rather than a Flatcoat or a Golden. Indeed I have known some quite disastrous results from Labrador to Whippet matings where the sole effect of the Whippet in the breeding makeup appeared to be to diminish the retriever size, so that one wound up with something like a miniature retriever. Unfortunately such dogs frequently seem to have a tendency to obesity, perhaps by reason of their not being of much use for any purpose and therefore unworked and under exercised. Greyhound to retriever crosses, whilst seldom displaying characteristics quite so distressing as these, nevertheless do have a tendency towards cloddiness and a general lack of that sort of build that one would be looking for in a lurcher.

SECOND CROSSES

The backcross of one of these first cross animals to the Greyhound usually produces useful dogs and there were a few of these on some of the Lincolnshire Wold farms at one time, which were well capable of coming to terms with the strong old hares which seemed to do so well on the limestone. As might have been expected they took little in the way of training to become good at retrieving their catches and would take hedge and ditch literally in their stride. I never heard of any of them being worked to a gate net and would not expect them to show up as well as the collie cross, with its inbuilt herding instincts, at this kind of work. One farmer, whom I knew quite well up there, an ex-cavalryman and a fearless rider to hounds with Lord Yarborough's Brocklesby pack, had two of these lurchers, which together with a Dachshund, he always had with him when he was riding around his farm. Between them they worked all the hedgerows on the place and kept his rabbits fairly well under control even in those premyxamatosis days. Like both their Labrador and Greyhound ancestors, such dogs can be rather strong willed and need to be trained with a certain degree of firmness.

THE FLATCOAT RETRIEVER

In order to find Flatcoated Retrievers round there in those days one had to go over the River Trent on to the Isle of Axholme. A very good strain of these dogs was maintained by the late Jonathan Batty of Amcotts, an old friend of my father. They were exceedingly hardy dogs being taken by their owner for a swim in the tidal stretches of the river every morning without fail in both winter and summer. At that time there was a very well supported coursing club on the Isle and both canine and human nature being what it is, some handy Flatcoat cross Greyhound lurchers were to be seen upon occasion. Of these I never saw anything beyond the first cross. These did not seem to turn out with the same heaviness as resulted when the Labrador formed the retriever part of the mix. Some of these dogs proved to be a bit self-willed, more so than the Labrador crosses in fact, but, apart from this little failing, were just about ideal for that land of river and warp and dyke. Most of the inhabitants were directly descended from the Commoners of the Isle who had so strongly resented the efforts of Vermuyden and his men to drain the watery wilderness which had existed until he had arrived there in the seventeenth century. They had made their livings mainly by fowling and fishing and had reacted violently against what they considered to be the intrusion of the Dutchmen, demonstrating their feelings by murdering many of the drainers and disposing of their remains in watery graves.

Martyn Huxley's Labrador/Greyhound cross.

THE GOLDEN RETRIEVER

Later on when I went to Norfolk for a couple of years I came across lurchers which were produced by crossing the Greyhound with the Golden Retriever, 'the showy golden' as the handsome creature had been called by imbedded reactionaires in the shooting field. If anything, I would say that these are a good deal more biddable than the other retriever crosses. They are, on the whole, friendly and good natured dogs although when one does happen to drop across a villain of this breeding, he can be expected to go the whole hog for their hides are so thick and proof against almost anything that it is not at all easy to make much of an impression on them once their minds are made up. There is little doubt in my own mind that the so-called Norfolk lurcher of the past was of this breeding, whatever their afficionados may say. The wheaten coloration of many of these dogs would also lend weight to the argument.

THE SPANIEL

I had not encountered much in the way of Spaniel blooded lurchers until quite recently when someone that I know acquired one. I understand that it was not the result of any sort of planned mating but rather in the nature of a byblow from the kennel of quite a well-known Whippet breeder. Although its owner had high hopes of it, I understand that these have not come to fruition. Having spent a good deal of time in my youth in the company of gamekeepers of the old school, I have no high opinion of Spaniels, which many of my old friends regarded as being foibles of the gentry produced with the sole purpose of making more difficult the lot of the hardworked keeper. This may be nothing more than old-fashioned prejudice but judging by the one example of this sort of lurcher which is available to me, I have seen nothing which might make me alter my opinion.

THE SETTER

Much the same sort of considerations apply to Setter blooded lurchers, the Setter in effect being nothing much more than a longlegged Spaniel. Setters, particularly of the Irish variety can be a bit of a handful sometimes. I once got as far as looking at a litter of these handsome animals with it in my mind that I might possibly purchase one. They had been bred by Father Maclennan at Hope Castle just on the outskirts of Castleblayney in County Monaghan. He seemed to look upon my request to view them outside of their quarters in a stable without a great deal of enthusiasm, and as soon as he opened the door I understood why for they were not to be seen for dust as they high tailed it for the border. I never discovered whether they caused an international incident by proceeding at full speed from the Republic to Northern Ireland for I did not stay there to find out. The last that I saw of the incident was the departure of the good Father together with two aged nuns whom he had apparently coopted as assistants, in hot pursuit of the errant animals in his ancient Ford Anglia. I meanwhile was cravenly making good my exit from the scene in the opposite direction.

They were useful sorts all right and, as they had so readily demonstrated, possessed a fair turn of speed, but I would not have fancied trying to train them to stay at home let alone anything else. Maybe their breeder, as a priest knew something which I did not about controlling them. He was a clerical gentleman of the good old sporting type and maintained a very good stock of pheasants during his time at Hope Castle. However, this was enough for me to decide that I would be unlikely to want a Setter as a gundog for they strike me as being rather flighty. Not good material for lurcher breeding either I am bound to believe. I believe the less common Irish Red and White Setter might be the better bet than the Irish Setter for anyone contemplating this cross.

THE RETRIEVER/SALUKI

To the best of my knowledge I had not encountered a gundog lurcher for quite a few years even at lurcher shows, where one is apt to drop across lurchers of all shapes, size and condition, until the other day when a young chap, whom I vaguely know, was walking past my house with what struck me as being a most useful looking dog. Knowing he has a good eye for the right sort, I asked him what it was. According to him it was carrying Labrador, Greyhound and of all things, Saluki blood in the proportion of ¼ Retriever, ¼ Saluki and ½ Greyhound. Although obviously a young dog, it was walking sedately at heel without benefit of a lead despite the presence of a lively terrier and the fact that its owner's young son was tearing around and letting off steam as kids of that age will. I am furthermore informed that it displays none of the usual Saluki vices.

Now that the corn is down I expect to see it put through its paces and shall be keeping an extremely wary eye on it as far as livestock is concerned. I can be fairly confident that it is all right with domestic poultry for I tested it out on some of my own there and then; I can only hope that it will be the same with sheep for, if it lives up to the promise, it looks like being a winner. Perhaps in this particular instance some of the less desirable Labrador and Saluki genes have cancelled one another out to some extent, but whether one would bring this off a second time may, of course, be a different matter.

Both sire and dam are available and having checked up on both of these, I feel reasonably sure that the version of the breeding which I have been given, is correct. Although this is probably only one of those million to one chances which has come off in lurcher breeding, it would be interesting to see how things turned out on a subsequent mating. Meanwhile I am beginning to revise a few of the opinions which I have previously held concerning the Saluki crosses for this may conceivably be the answer. Should it be possible to ameliorate its undesirable characteristics in some way, this could prove to be something for which many of us have been searching, something which, in lurcher breeding usually seems to be about as unattainable as the Philosopher's Stone. In theory, I can think of no better way of doing it than by the introduction of retriever blood; a collie input would, I think, merely tend to accentuate many of the traits which we dislike in Salukis.

CONCLUSION

There is one very good reason why a retriever of any sort is a useful component in any kind of lurcher breeding, this being that it is still possible to find plenty of working dogs of these breeds, one which has not been turned over entirely to the production of dog show winners at any price. Just as in the case of collie lurchers it is advisable when enquiring into the blood lines behind any gundog lurcher to ensure that the non-Greyhound part of the mix is from a working strain. Unlike the sheepdog, however, a retriever has a further factor in its favour, that field trial dogs remain good all round working dogs, some of the best of them in fact, whereas the same can scarcely be said of the sheep dog trial collie, which whilst being a winner at pushing five sheep around a course and finally penning them, all of this being carried out under close supervision, may not be quite so good when it comes to showing what it can do as an all round working dog. It is thus possible to find the best retriever blood lines without too much difficulty.

Should someone take it into his head to produce lurchers, using a Labrador Retriever and Greyhound cross or a Flatcoat and Greyhound cross, and give to his breeding programme the same amount of care and attention which goes into the breeding of certain collie lurcher products, I am quite sure that the results would be equally good if not better than many of the collie lurchers.

Of the retrievers which are available I would on the whole be inclined to favour the Flatcoat for the production of lurchers where this breed's setting ancestry and consequent inbred motivation to quest might be expected to manifest itself to advantage.

Guard Dog Crosses

Leaving out anything which is completely exotic, there are three breeds of dog which can be described as purpose bred guard dogs and these are the Alsatian, now generally referred to as the German Shepherd; the Doberman and the Rottweiller.

THE ROTTWEILLER

Of these three breeds I think that for purposes of lurcher breeding we can write off the Rottweiller immediately. They are big heavy dogs, even cuddly in appearance, although far from this in nature, and from the sheer point of conformation would never do as part of the makeup of any sort of lurcher. I know that there are all sorts of tales about their being drovers' dogs. As soon as the drover had delivered his fourfooted bovine wares to their destination, he was said to have placed the money which he received for his beef on the hoof, inside some special pocket within the dog's collar. He then despatched it homewards so that should he be set upon by footpads, he would have no cash about him. Quite apart from any of the muggers, who were not completely bereft of intelligence, giving the dog its quietus with the nearest handy blunderbuss or horse pistol, and then stealing the drover's hard won cash, there is the added point that in those days, cheques and even banknotes were not in use as currency. The dog would have had to carry just about its own weight in gold in order to perform this unlikely transfer of funds. No, this story is strictly for the birds, along with other unlikely tales about the Golden Retriever having been started off by Lord Tweedsdale's purchasing a likely looking dog from a cobbler, he having acquired his stock from the performing dogs of some Russian circus, and the equally unlikely one of some Polish sea captain named Grabski swapping the ancestors of today's Bearded Collies for Scottish sheep.

THE DOBERMAN

This leaves us with the other two breeds and, in theory, the Doberman would seem to be absolutely ideal material for providing the non-sighthound side of the lurcher combination. This is a fascinating breed. It came into existence in about 1890 when it was founded by Herr Louis Doberman of Apolda in Thuringia, this being part of what became the East German Republic. His bitch, Schnupp, was registered as No 1 in the first Stud Book of the Doberman Pinscher Club of Germany. The breed is reputed to have come into existence by crossing the Pinscher, the Weimaraner Pointer and some sort of Vorstenhund. The Rottweiller is also thought to have perhaps been used, and mention has also been made of the Manchester Terrier being brought in.

As well as being a very competent dog breeder, Doberman followed the occupation of rat and rabbit catcher and it was for use in this capacity that he originally created the breed. It is on record that his original Doberman Pinscher was a very different sort of animal from that which we know today, being described as prick eared, smaller and less smooth of coat. In fact it sounds as though it must have been something on the lines of a small lurcher.

The breed was never a large one at its inception and, in fact, faced virtual extinction in the early years of this century when, in 1910, Herr Otto Goller took the breed in hand, smartened it up considerably and turned it into the dog which it is today. These dogs have since become widely used as police and tracker dogs.

At first sight this would appear to be a perfect part of the lurcher makeup with its excellent abilities for tracking and obedience trials, plus the background of its original pest control function. One occasionally encounters the odd lurcher which has been bred as a Doberman/Greyhound cross and one wonders why there are not more of them.

One reason for this, I think, must be the unenviable reputation which the Doberman seems to have acquired for sometimes turning on its handler during moments of stress, and this would certainly tend to put many people off having a lurcher of this breeding. However, although one sees so few of them that it is difficult to form an opinion, the reason may well lie elsewhere. One reason could well be how true such a cross might be expected to breed.

In other respects, including that of size, the average Doberman being about 25 inches in height and 45 pounds weight, the union with a Greyhound might seem to be the basis for a very useful sort of lurcher.

The dog very much resembles a large sized Manchester Terrier and some years ago I encountered someone who was the proud possessor of what he claimed to be two Miniature Dobermans. This was at a time when there seemed to be a miniature version, usually brought about by inbreeding to runts, of just about every breed of dog there was and someone appeared to have decided to cash in on both the popularity of Dobermans and of miniature dogs. Something did not ring quite true about them, however, for they had a great deal more guts and gumption about them than the average miniature, or for that matter, some of the Dobermans which one sees. It suddenly hit me that these were Manchester Terriers which had been given a Doberman style dock.

THE ALSATIAN

This leaves us with the Alsatian cross; I still prefer to call them Alsatians

German Shepherd/Greyhound Lurcher owned by John Hancock.

rather than German Shepherd Dogs for this is what they were called during the formative years of my life. This was at the time after the 1914–18 War when any German connection was anathema to so many people, a hangover from a wartime phobia mainly fostered by those who took no active part in the hostilities. There are quite a number of lurchers of this cross about and those people who have them always seem to be well pleased with them.

The problem is finding a suitable Alsatian these days due to the changes made to them by the show people. There have been various troubles with the breed in recent years, the most serious of these being a good deal of hip dysplasia but this is unlikely to appear in the outcross. All the same, if I were to be producing this sort of lurcher, I would endeavour to breed to Alsatians of recent importation for the German breed society has adopted a very rigid code whereby such ailments are more or less unknown there.

On the first cross, lurchers of this breeding tend to be rather heavy, and most of the very useful ones which I have seen have been of the three-quarters cross. This produces a much more lithe and agile sort of dog. One of my farming neighbours always has a lurcher of this sort replacing like with like. Both he and his good lady are phenomenally good producers of both hunters and racehorses and I have usually found that when a person has a good eye for a horse, he or she has a good one for a dog as well.

The Alsatian is really the only one of the crosses to guard dog breeds that one could recommend with confidence but I would not mind giving the Doberman lurcher a try for all that. I have a feeling that if one got hold of the right one, it could prove to be an absolute winner in the right hands. I lay accent on the right hands for such a dog would almost certainly be inclined to being headstrong.

CONCLUSION

The Alsatian cross might well appeal to the enthusiast looking for an all round lurcher who feels the collie cross is not quite what he is looking for. It is a cross that is unlikely to appeal to the keen show enthusiast but is worth looking at if you want a working lurcher.

Other Breeds and Crosses

From time to time one meets with rather unusual crossbreeds which, although somewhat out of the ordinary, are nonetheless lurchers. I suspect that the majority of these have arrived on the scene rather by happenstance than by design. The subject of the book, *Rebecca the Lurcher* (Andrew Simpson, 1973, Barrie & Jenkins) was described as being a Foxhound/Greyhound cross; this may have accounted for her seemingly marked degree of intractability.

From time to time one sees unusual sorts of lurchers being advertised. As well as these, the wicked world being what it is, I would hazard the opinion that a certain number of the others advertised are not what they are said to be. For instance any astute and not over scrupulous owner of a longdog bitch which manages to get itself in whelp to a poodle, would not have much difficulty in passing off the offspring as being of Bedlington blood.

IBIZAN AND PHAROAH HOUNDS

Certain pure breeds of dog exist which themselves are lurcherlike both in conformation and in performance. Amongst these the Mediterranean breeds of hunting dog, in particular the Eivissenc, which is known in Britain as the Ibizan Hound, is worthy of note. The Ibizan Hound is of typical longdog shape except that it usually has prick ears; it is a very fast mover. It is a breed of some antiquity and is claimed to have been brought to the Balearic Islands and the east coast of Spain, where it is mainly to be found, by the Phoenicians. They were first seen in England at Cruft's in 1929 when Mr J Charpy imported two of them from Spain. Since then more have come in and in 1988 at the same event no less than 47 were on display, the same number incidentally as the very similar Pharoah Hound.

In their native lands these dogs are mainly used for hunting rabbits. They are natural jumpers and are not difficult to teach to retrieve to hand. As well as possessing a fair turn of speed and agility they have a marked degree of stamina. Why then, particularly since being a pure breed, they may be relied upon to breed true, are they not more popular in Britain as a hunting dog? There is one good reason for this and it is that they give tongue whilst hunting. This will, of course, damn them in the eyes of the majority of lurcher owners since, quite apart from other considerations, this sort of behaviour can be relied upon to put the game to ground in double quick time. I believe that there are one or two people who have crossed Ibizan Hounds and also Pharoah Hounds with Greyhounds and those, about which I have heard anything, are reported as being satisfactory. But why go to this sort of trouble when proven types of lurcher already exist? I suppose it is the age old thing about wanting to see what is on the other side of the hill and as such can only be applauded for this is what exploration and the adventurous life is all about.

Whereas the numbers of such dogs which are being exhibited at Cruft's and similar dog shows is steadily on the increase, I have yet to see one of their number or indeed any sort of crossbred bred from them, shown at any lurcher show which I have attended either in official or unofficial capacity.

Other dogs of a vaguely similar sort exist in the Spanish Galgo and the Portuguese Podengo. So far as I know none of these ever appear at British dog shows of any kind, which merely indicates that to date no one has seen the possibility of making a fast buck out of breeding them. By the same token neither do they put in their appearance at lurcher shows. Like their Ibizan and Pharoah Hound relatives they may also be relied upon to open up on quarry.

Various suggestions are put forward from time to time about some of the continental sheep and cattle dogs being in some way of roughly similar blood to the legendary Smithfield, but I have yet to see any sort of lurcher which might have carried this sort of blood. Having had a fleeting acquaintance with a Bouvier de Flandre (Belgian Cattle Dog) I do not know that I should want to do so either.

THE LURCHER/LURCHER

Much if not the majority of lurcher production is the result of lurcher to lurcher breeding. There is no doubt that some very useful dogs emerge

John Bayles Lurcher dog, Tip, bred from five generations of Lurcher to Lurcher matings.

from the litters bred by such unions but every pup from one of these matings is an imponderable in itself. Usually the owner only has a sketchy idea, at best, of his dog's pedigree and the various crosses that have gone into its making. Often there is such a mixture of ancestral virtues and vices wandering around in the systems of such animals that as a result of mating any two of them, no matter how promising they may seem to be, just about anything may emerge.

Many quite good looking dogs, who are also good performers in the field, can not honestly be described as anything other than mongrels. You may hear about those whose lines are said to breed true, but such breeders would have a bit of a job on their hands to make any sort of accurate forecast as to what their next litter is going to be like. Some mongrel lurchers are very, very good indeed but it must be remembered that such breeding is unpredictable and you could just as easily breed or buy the pup that proves to be useless. Even when one is absolutely certain of the lines behind any particular dog it is difficult enough predicting the outcome once more than two strains, let alone two breeds, are involved. It is quite possible to demonstrate the probabilities of just about any combination of genes as the result of any matings but, since I do not feel that there is a place for any quasi-scientific mumbojumbo in a book of this nature, I do not intend to pursue the matter in that particular direction. A moment or two's serious consideration, though, must lead anyone to the conclusion that results must be far from finite. So why complicate the issue by venturing into the realms of the indeterminate when there are dogs to be had where there is a fair chance of the animal turning out to be something in the nature of what you had expected it to be?

— 5 —
Longdogs

By the term 'Longdogs' I refer to those hounds of the chase which pursue their quarry by using their sight, rather than by using their noses as is the way of hunting in the case of Foxhounds, Beagles, Otterhounds, Harriers, Staghounds and their like. It may be noted that I have said that longdogs use their eyes *rather* than their noses and I have advisedly put it this way for many longdogs are possessed of excellent scenting powers. However, since their sight is considerably superior to that of most other dogs they prefer not to use the latter faculty until such time as they become unsighted of their quarry. Many of them will be seen at that moment to start to get their noses down and their scenting powers should be in no way despised. My own Greyhound/Deerhound hybrids are very good in this respect and I would consider them to be the equal of many gundogs at sniffing out their quarry when no other means seems to be available. Like everything else, scenting ability is usually a matter of training a dog to use those senses with which it happens to be blessed. No Bloodhound would go very far in pursuit of the clean boot if it were not trained to the job. Likewise with the matter of retrieving to hand; many longdogs or sighthounds, call them what you will, take quite naturally to retrieving if introduced to it at a sufficiently early age.

So why, may you ask, bother to go to the trouble of crossing these paragons of canine ability with anything else? This is, as they say, a good question to which the answer has to be that we produce lurchers in order to provide that little bit extra which each of us as an individual requires in his perfect dog. The man who worked a gate net needed a dog which would herd its quarry towards him and the net so that he added some collie to the longdog; he who required his hound to swim through the drains and levels of Fenland would introduce retriever blood and so it went on. Mind you, all these ideas are all very well in theory but the results do not always come out quite as might have been anticipated. As I have mentioned previously, blessed is he who expecteth nothing for he shall not be disappointed. And there have been plenty of disappointments in lurcher breeding with the results not matching up to either of their parents. One is reminded of the letter which was reputed to have been sent from Mrs Patrick Campbell to George Bernard Shaw proposing that they should have a child together since this might be expected to possess the Shavian brain and Mrs Campbell's looks. Reply came there from G.B.S. saying that he would not countenance such a thing since in all probability the unfortunate infant would have its father's looks and its mother's brain. However it is better, they tell us, to travel in hope than to actually arrive and this attitude of mind explains quite a lot about lurcher breeding.

To get back to the subject of longdogs, as I explained in the introduction to this book, the term includes such dogs as Greyhounds, Wolfhounds, Whippets, Salukis, Afghans, Deerhounds, Borzois and the crosses between these breeds. Of these for the purposes of lurcher breeding we can immediately rule out the Afghan, the Irish Wolfhound and the Borzoi since they are just too big to be used on any game which is regularly hunted in this country. Apart from this the Afghan and the Borzoi are both remarkably low in their I.Q.s, and the Irish Wolfhound has been so altered by the breeders from the dog which was developed by Captain Graham a century or more ago that its conformation is completely wrong from the lurcher breeder's point of view. This leaves us with the Greyhound, the Whippet, the Deerhound and the Saluki all of which possesses to greater or lesser degree some characteristics which will prove to be of interest as a basis for lurcher production. Let us have a look at these breeds in a bit more detail.

THE GREYHOUND

In any choice of a Greyhound for lurcher breeding I always like to know the animal pretty well before using it. Just any old Greyhound, be it of either track or coursing blood, will not do, the reason being that I will be looking for a sensible, thinking sort of dog. In my experience the brain power of individual Greyhounds tends to differ to a very marked extent as does their temperament. Some of their number seem to be capable of reasoned, rational sort of thought and are able to size up any situation, working it out so as to tackle it in the way which appears to be most

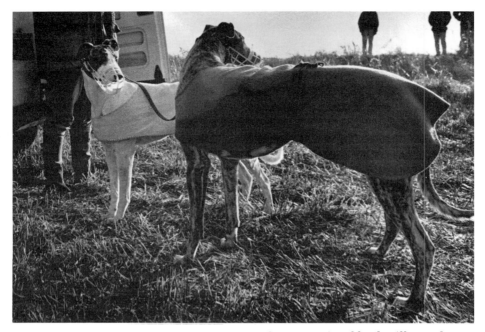

Just any old Greyhound, be it of either track or coursing blood will not do ...,
Greyhounds waiting their turn at The Altcar 1000 Meeting.

suitable in its mind; others just seem to be a bit thick and short on brains. In the matter of temperament the situation is a very similar one; one dog will be of kindly disposition whilst another will be aggressive and looking for trouble. Odd ones, fortunately few in number, are just downright savage. So it pays to look around for a while until you find the right one. My preference is for an animal which has proved itself to be able to use its brains on the track and later on has been used in competitive coursing under rules where it has displayed an equal amount of common sense.

I have found quite a number of dogs in this way which will measure up to my parameters; a bit of quiet and above all unbiased observation will soon show you the one which you want. Those which make a habit of placing themselves advantageously on the track and beat their opponents on the run up and then dominate the scene on the coursing field are the dogs from which to breed. Observe their demeanour when off the track as well; it does not take long to find the one with that little bit extra going for it. My favourite stud dog of all time, as well as proving himself no fool on either track or field, would always try to sneak into my car in the hopes of a free trip with a good run at the end of it whenever I paid its owner a visit. He left me the best running dog pups which I have ever bred.

Do not be overinsistent on a Greyhound being exclusively of coursing blood. They were all of coursing strain until the introduction of Greyhound racing tracks in the 1920s and the dogs used for the two different branches of sport are not all that far apart even today. To my mind not sufficiently far as to make very much difference when crossed with another breed of dog. Given the choice between a sensible track dog and a coursing animal which appeared to be none too bright, no matter how purple its pedigree, my preference would without hesitation be given to the track Greyhound.

Above all do not give too much credence to the tales which one is apt to hear about the Greyhound being some sort of brainless moron. As I have mentioned, some are a good deal brighter than others but it is also possible to find unintelligent lurchers and, despite claims to the contrary, rather dim collies and gundogs. Like all longdogs, Greyhounds usually require considerably more in the way of training than do intelligent dogs of other breeds but for anyone who is willing and who has the opportunity to put in the time and effort which is needed in the job of schooling, the results can be surprisingly satisfactory.

THE WHIPPET

I have found the majority of Whippets to be amongst the most intelligent of all the longdog breeds. On the whole it is not so necessary to look as hard at their antecedents as when one is breeding to Greyhound blood. However, look one should for undesirable specimens exist within every breed and every species. The one drawback which the Whippet has is its size, making it only really suitable for working rat and rabbit. Given a short slip a Whippet can catch a hare, but this can not be thought of as its main function. It is also possible for one to kill a fox, but it would not be right to regard such a dog as being primarily a fox killer. Because of its size one has to be very careful for the last thing that anyone should want is for his Whippet to become involved in any sort of fox versus dog fight. However, matched to the correct sort of quarry, rabbit and rat, a Whippet will often give a better account of itself than many other sorts of dog. It can be seen at its best in daytime rabbiting where, as a ferreter's companion, it has very few equals. Many of them also excel as bushing dogs where, despite their thin skins, they can be relied upon to get into thick undergrowth, push out their rabbits, then course and kill them in the open. Properly entered to rat they will often prove to be the equal of many a terrier.

In lurcher breeding, Whippets are frequently crossed with Bedlingtons, the resultant offspring from the first cross being quite typey as a rule and enjoying a ready sale. Crossed with other breeds such as collies and gundogs they are better taken to the three-quarter breeding since the half breds usually grow out as heavy, blocky dogs. In my time I have seen quite

A fine looking coursing Whippet.

a number of Whippet lurchers of various sorts but, on the whole, I would say that the pure bred Whippet was the better and more useful dog.

In its outcrosses to Greyhounds the Whippet has produced many handy dogs which were much esteemed in the old days of flapping tracks and early Whippet racing, when not quite so much emphasis was placed upon the purity of breeding of the competing dogs. Such crossbreds have also been deservedly popular as working animals although one does not see so many of them about these days; but then how many of the old sorts of running dog does one see today with so many people having gone over to the collie crosses?

Whippet/Greyhounds are sometimes used in lurcher breeding being put to some other dog such as a sheepdog or a gundog, but when engaging in this kind of breeding one must be prepared to cull hard. Dogs in the resultant litters are quite likely to be of various shapes and sizes, favouring their Whippet ancestors in one case, the Greyhound in another and the sheepdog or whatever was used in others with very little in the middle, thus more or less missing the original object of the exercise.

Whilst Whippet to Greyhound crosses can be very good indeed, the crossing of Whippets with larger dogs, such as collies and gundogs can sometimes lead to disappointing results. Unless a breeder has had a good deal of experience with such dogs, the use of Whippets for lurcher breeding is, in my opinion, best left alone and, should there be any intention of the perpetuation of such a line of lurchers, Whippet blood should not be introduced at all.

THE DEERHOUND

In the Deerhound we have a pure bred that I regard as being pretty near to the ideal all round running dog. Although not all of them are as good as they used to be when their main purpose was the pursuit of the Red Deer, there are still plenty of good ones amongst them. The working qualities have been maintained by the Deerhound coursing meetings which are regularly held in both Scotland and the Fens. Dogs of this breed seem to possess that bit more intelligence and seem to accept training better than

Cloud, a purebred Deerhound bitch and marvellous worker.

59

most other longdogs, excepting perhaps the Whippet. The only criticism that I have of them is that for allround use they are rather too large. This coupled with the conformation of their necks, which in Deerhounds are shorter and stronger than those of the Greyhound, the dog having been evolved to deal with heavier quarry, makes Deerhounds inclined to fail to some extent on the pickup. The surest way of remedying this is to use a Greyhound/Deerhound crossbred employing the smaller type of animals on both sides of the mating. A small track Greyhound is ideal and it is possible to find smallish Deerhounds if one looks around a bit for them. By a small Deerhound I mean a dog of 28 inches or a bitch of 26 inches. Such animals do exist although those Deerhound breeders who are keen on showing their dogs have rather tended to set their faces against them. They are most easily found amongst animals from those kennels where the main object is coursing. I have used this sort of dog for some years now and have not discovered them to be wanting in any way.

THE SALUKI

Salukis are of fairly recent introduction compared with Greyhounds, Deerhounds and Whippets, but they have certainly made their mark in the field of competitive coursing of 'the best of three' variety proving themselves as successful hare killers both as pure breds and when crossed with the Greyhound. This however is a specialised area of field sports and does no more than demonstrate that a particular type of dog excels at this single kind of activity. Until a few years ago Deerhound crosses were favoured for this sort of event but they have also shown their worth at other work, which is more than can be said for the Saluki. This is a pity for Salukis are personable dogs and are the right shape and size to make an allround running dog. The trouble lies within their elegant craniums for they all seem to be a bit short on sense, this being not much improved by crossing them to the Greyhound.

Whilst the Saluki has been recognised for the canine athlete which it undoubtedly is, possessing limitless stamina although lacking the Greyhound's initial burst of speed, I feel that it has not been fully tested as a possible cross for breeding lurchers. Whenever it has formed part of a cross breeding programme to anything other than a pure bred Greyhound there always seems to be some collie blood in the mix. To my mind, this has done nothing but accentuate the Salukis reputation for being unsteady with farm livestock. It is well known amongst sheep men, of whose number I count myself, having had charge of very large flocks all over the place from the north of England to the tropics, that a collie which happens to be a wrong'un can be one of the most tiresome sheep worriers that it is possible to find. Ally this sort of blood to that of a dog which itself is not to be trusted in the presence of livestock, such as the Saluki, and this

Some Salukis will retrieve.

becomes an instant recipe for trouble. Just as soon as more people get hold of the idea that the way to introduce Saluki blood into the lurcher mix is by means of allying it to something steady, such as a retriever, the sooner will the Saluki stand some chance of rehabilitation on the score of reliability. This is yet another facet of the problems which have been caused by the constant propagandising of the collie lurcher, sometimes seemingly past the point of reason, so that to many lurchermen any dog without collie blood in it is somehow no longer a lurcher.

CONCLUSION

The four breeds of longdog which I have described are, in my opinion, the only ones which it is reasonable to consider in the context of lurcher breeding. The remainder, Afghans, Borzois and the like do not really merit serious consideration, but anyone who is interested in such dogs will find that I have had a certain amount to say about them in my earlier book, *The Working Longdog* (1989, Dickson Price), to which I would refer them.

For those interested in showing, the cross between two purebred longdogs is very popular. Such crosses not only produce sensational lookers but the offspring from such a mating is pretty predictable.

— 6 —
The Puppy: Choosing, Rearing and Training

Choosing

What sort of lurcher do you want? Or more to the point what sort of lurcher do you require? This is not always quite the same thing and perhaps merits a rather greater degree of consideration for the choices are many. You may need a dog which can take hares, you may need one for lamping rabbits at night, for catching ferreted ones, for bushing them by day, one for controlling foxes or for yet some other purpose. You may have in mind something that so looks the part that it will be awarded rosettes at lurcher shows, whilst on the other hand you may seek a dog that will not be readily recognisable as the running dog which it actually is. There is one great advantage about choosing a lurcher; this is the fact that lurchers may be produced to suit pretty near all requirements and conditions. Not only may they be bred for specific purposes but many of them are extremely versatile in their individual capabilities. Here are a few indications of which sort of lurcher may be expected to do what sort of job.

HARE

Nowadays, there are fewer people who require a dog to take a hare for hares are no longer looked upon as food to keep a working man's family in meat for a week, as they formerly were. Nor are they so readily caught in these days of prairie farming with so few hedges and places wherein to set

A Saluki/Greyhound.

a net. Some sort of dog which could be relied upon to herd quarry into a net was needed then but now when we speak of a hare dog we are thinking of an entirely different creature, one with no herding ability but with the speed to come to terms with its fleeting quarry, together with the cunning to lay off and catch it as it turns. Should you need such a dog you will probably be thinking not of lurchers but of longdogs, dogs with Saluki or Deerhound blood mingled with that of the Greyhound. The less of any other sort of breed that there is about the dog the better . . . For anyone who is interested in the longdog as opposed to the lurcher I should mention that I have covered such matters at considerably greater length in my earlier book, *The Working Longdog*. If you are in a part of the country where you are still so fortunate as to have a few spots where a net might be set then this will be one of the locations in which a dog with collie blood *of the right kind* might be preferable. This crossed with Greyhound or Whippet to the half or three-quarter cross would probably do quite well.

RABBIT

If the hare was the lurcherman's main quarry of yesteryear then the rabbit can be said to be today's staple. The basic purpose of the lurcher

There are likely to be more of them just as long as the present rate of recovery from the filthy disease Myxomatosis keeps going . . .

remains the same, that of keeping filled the cooking pot, nowadays usually known as a casserole. In present times there is no better way of accomplishing this than to have a dog which is adept at catching rabbits for amongst wild game, these are available in larger numbers than anything else. There are likely to be even more of them just as long as the present rate of recovery from the filthy disease of myxomatosis keeps going and the evil boffins do not come up with something even nastier.

Your choice of dog will depend to a greater extent on how many rabbits you will want to take and the acreage of ground over which you intend to hunt. If you are likely to be thinking in terms of large numbers then it is extremely probable that you will be taking them on the lamp. You will, therefore, require some sort of dog which is capable of catching its quarry on the beam, and this being so, you are to a certain extent in luck for a good many dogs are capable of carrying out this sort of work. It is by no means necessary for a dog to have any great turn of speed to score at lamping rabbits, and indeed there are dogs with no longdog blood at all in their veins which are capable of the job. What is of considerably greater importance is that the chosen dog should have plenty of stamina, and indeed stamina to spare, for upon this will depend the number of runs which it is able to make in a night's work and, in consequence, the size of your bag. This fairly effectively rules out the use of small lurchers, the Whippet crosses, for whilst most of these, including pure bred Whippets, are absolutely ace at getting off to a flying start and can, moreover, be relied upon to pick up a rabbit just as effectively when in pursuit of one on the beam as by any other means, there cannot exist much doubt that such a dog would not be able to match the overall stamina of the larger dogs.

Just about any sort of cross between the Greyhound and the collie or one of the larger terriers such as an Airedale or a Bedlington or an Irish Terrier will have it well within its capabilities to cope with this sort of work

For daytime rabbiting the Bedlington/Whippet is currently much favoured.

and gundog and Alsatian crosses can be just as good. Just as long as any of these are from good working strains they will have sufficient reserves of strength to keep going for quite an appreciable length of time, and should also have quite enough in the way of speed to be master of most situations.

Apart from the importance of stamina there is also the matter of being able to take in their stride the generality of obstacles which they may encounter in the course of a night's work. Whereas the Greyhound bred lurcher, assuming that it has been properly trained, can be relied upon to sail over the normal stock proof fence with plenty of room to spare between it and the top length of wire, most small lurchers will not be quite able to make it and will have to be lifted over. As well as being tiresome and becoming more so with each repetition, this is also apt to be time wasting and unproductive.

For daytime rabbiting such as bushing and working to ferrets many of the small lurchers can be quite adequate with the Bedlington/Whippet cross being currently very much favoured. A dog for this sort of work should, unlike its lamping counterpart, be possessed of a good nose for both valuable time and effort are wasted by putting a ferret down a hole when the rabbits are not at home. The terrier/Greyhound crosses are useful at this style of hunting although perhaps they may not have just that lightning degree of acceleration which is the trademark of the Whippet. For bushing a similar sort of dog to the ferreting helpmate is required, something with a good sense of smell and the ability to get off its mark without any hesitation. As well as this it should be of a size to be able to negotiate bramble bushes and hedgebottoms, thus dispensing with the necessity of using a terrier to bolt the game. Plenty of pure bred Whippets are adept at this and, in theory, a Whippet cross with a stronger coat and a thicker skin than the pure blooded article should be even better at the job. In practice though, I have found the straight Whippet to be able to cope with this sort of work equally as well if not a trifle better than the crossbred.

FOX

If you are taking rabbits with the lamp you will already be tooled up for the job. You have the lamp, you have the dog, you have the land over which to hunt and it is reasonable to believe that in most cases less fox will mean more rabbit. Foxes are notorious killers of small and defenceless creatures, not the least of which are young rabbits and hares. So it would seem to be a pity to stop at rabbit when there is fox to be had as well. For this you will have to be a bit more careful in your choice of a lurcher than you would have been, had you had only rabbits in mind.

Personally I use Deerhound hybrids for this kind of work. Such dogs deal with fox without much hassle and have the stamina to seemingly go on for ever. Certainly it well outlasts my own. I would, therefore, always recommend a certain amount of Deerhound blood in any lurcher which was to be used primarily for this purpose. Some collie bred animals are capable of dealing with fox but others are not and, I regret to say sometimes exhibit a somewhat craven attitude towards them. Anything with the right sort of terrier blood about it will usually prove itself master of the situation and many are clean killers of fox without appearing to use much effort.

SHOWING

Despite whatever they may say to the contrary many owners today hardly ever work their dogs, their main interest being in the summer lurcher shows. Should you be in the business of hunting rosettes rather than rabbits then you will have to consider the best way of catching the judge's eye instead of catching next week's dinner. What is the best way of accomplishing this? The main thing which you will require will be an eye catching dog, something that looks the part of the archetypal lurcher as it exists in the mind of the general public. In my opinion the quickest and surest way of doing this is to acquire a dog with plenty of Deerhound blood, enough to give it a broken coat for preference. In fact I know of at least one pure bred Deerhound which quite regularly is found to be well placed at lurcher shows. By the same token but rather less frequently, unadulterated Greyhounds are sometimes seen to be walking away with the awards although in my experience less frequently than their hairier cousins. How often does one hear the remark at the side of the judging ring to the effect that 'He isn't interested in anything that hasn't got a good look of Deerhound about it.' Of course there are some judges who do not favour broken coated dogs; they are often the ones who choose the Greyhounds.

But have no doubts about it, a few competitors at such events are deadly serious about the whole business of showing and can become quite peevish when their dogs are not placed as well as they had expected them to be. I must say, however, that the great majority of those taking part are very good humoured and look upon such events exactly as they were originally intended to be, a day out with a bit of fun thrown in.

NOW THINK CAREFULLY

If you have no experience of lurchers then you should think twice, or maybe even three times, before committing yourself to the ownership of what is a very special and in many ways, unusual type of canine.

If you have no intention of working your lurcher but intend keeping it as a pet, or perhaps for the purpose of exhibiting at one of the lurcher shows which are held all over the country during the summer months would you

Tom Hilden with Jessica.

not be better off with some other sort of dog? A lurcher is above all a working animal, one which has been devised and bred for work and which is much the better for having a certain amount of employment. A dog of this nature will gravitate towards making its own form of amusement, should it not be provided with sufficient to do, this not infrequently being attended with disastrous consequences, a ready example being that of stock worrying. In this connection it is as well to bear in mind the fact that lurchers are not, on the whole, as easy to confine as are many other breeds of dog for most of them can get over obstacles which are very high indeed as well as possessing considerable ability to tunnel underneath or indeed through them; their heads and necks are so formed as to render lurchers more adept than most dogs at slipping their collars and they are by no means slow to discover ways of biting through or otherwise making useless many kinds of tether. So novices be warned. Here is a dog which requires a good deal of exercise and work to keep it right not only in wind and limb but also in mind and, if you are not prepared to devote a good deal of your time to your dog, go for some other breed which may be easier to manage.

DOG OR BITCH

Once you have made the decision that a lurcher is the only dog for you what is the next move? Yet more decision making is looking you in the face. Do you want a dog or a bitch? Do you want a grown or part grown animal rather than a pup? What sort of breeding do you wish to have in the dog of your choice?

Let's take things in just that order and start off with the superiority of dogs over bitches or vice versa. There is an old saying which goes something like this; 'Why have a bitch which is a nuisance for three or four weeks twice a year when you can have a dog which is a nuisance all the time.' Yes, that's right; sex raises its ugly head yet again.

Nowadays drugs such as 'Ovarid' may be relied upon to reduce the period during which a bitch is in season from the best part of a month to a few days but this aspect of the matter apart, there are other reasons why many lurcher owners prefer the female to the male of the species, one of which is that they (bitches) have a reputation for being keener and more efficient hunters than dogs. I have used both sexes and, to be perfectly honest, have found neither of them wanting. Nevertheless, I have a theory at the back of my mind, for which I must admit there seems to be no cogent reason, that whereas bitches seem to do better for men, dogs often appear to work better for women. There is an old saying amongst the owners of coursing Greyhounds, 'Dogs are sprinters and bitches are stayers', but I have always thought by the twinkle in their eyes that a certain amount of sexual inuendo is intended!

There is, however, one utterly undeniable fact which is that in any one litter, the dogs will generally be larger and heavier in the bone than the bitches. This seems to me to be a point worth considering in that, should you be going in for one of the larger Greyhound based lurchers, then a female, being a lighter and handier animal, might be preferable, whilst in the case of the smaller Whippet crosses, a dog which will be of somewhat larger size, might better fill one's needs.

In the end, it all comes down to personal preferences and prejudices but, should you not be sure as to what you want in this respect, I would never advise anyone to seek the middle path by way of castrating a male or spaying a female lurcher. In either sex this procedure stands a fair chance of producing a distinct tendency to obesity and lack of drive, whilst, in the female, problems of incontinency not infrequently arise. Whatever apologia may be forthcoming on the part of those advocating such measures, never forget that the emasculation of farm livestock is carried out for the simple and straightforward reason that the animal fattens better and is more quiescent. These are not characteristics which many of us look for in a running dog.

The question of whether to have a dog or a bitch may, however, be decided for you. The pups in the litter which takes your eye may all be of that sex which you have decided not to have or, on inspecting a litter, the pup which you want may well turn out to be of the wrong sex. To my mind, the matter of whether to have a dog or a bitch does not assume any very great importance if this is to be, as I think it should be, your one and only lurcher. Should you already have a dog of any sort, however, then to acquire another one of the opposite sex is to provide yourself with a very great deal of trouble. I am aware that quite a number of lurcher owners do have animals of opposite sexes but I can only say that there would be a great deal less hassle in their lives if they did not do so.

A small number of novice dog owners with thoughts of breeding, and making large and easy profits from so doing, sometimes purchase a dog as well as a bitch. I would just say that unless you happen to be an experienced dog breeder with adequate kennel facilities at your disposal, you do not do it this way. Even if you happen to be such a breeder, you would still probably go outside your own kennel to find your stud dog.

FINDING A LURCHER

Having decided, or not decided as the case may be, on whether you prefer a dog or a bitch, the next thing is to find a lurcher for sale. There are usually quite a few of these on offer as a glance at the classified columns of *The Countryman's Weekly* will reveal. At this point there are more decisions to be made. Do you want a pup or do you want a grown or partly grown dog? Unless you are a skilled and experienced lurcher person it is by no means easy to forecast just what any particular pup in a litter, or for that matter the entire litter, is going to turn out like on achieving maturity. Even a skilled and experienced lurcher person, if she or he is entirely honest, will admit to having been wrong upon occasion.

So what do we do? The partly grown lurcher will show some pretty unmistakable indications of its conformation so that at any rate, you are going to know what it will look like. But is this enough? The answer to this one is that it most certainly is not. The matter of temperament has to be taken into account for it matters not a jot how good the dog's appearance is, if it happens to be a wrong'un. Which it will stand a pretty good chance of being, should you go in for an adult or sapling lurcher, and bad habits, or unsatisfactory outlook take a deal of effort to correct. My advice would be to always go for the pup unless you should just happen to know all that there is to be known about the background and the breeding of an adult dog.

Having decided that your best course is to acquire a pup, the next question is where to find one. Without much doubt the answer to this is to get the dog from some person whom you know and who happens to be breeding but, of course, this is an ideal state of affairs which occurs only too rarely. The next best option is to look for your pup somewhere close at hand, say from some breeder within your own or some adjoining county. In these days of lurcher shows and other similar social events most lurcher people are acquainted with others of like interests who reside within the same area. By all means, attend a few lurcher shows and you will not find it difficult to strike up conversation with lurcher owners who are present, but do not let any of them sell you a dog at this stage as this would be to completely defeat the object of the exercise. In this way you will not only be likely to hear a bit of 'in' gossip and get to know who is breeding what, but will also get your eye in as regards the sort of thing that you want. If any litters are being offered for sale locally, endeavour to get to know all that you can about them before arranging to view the pups.

I would advise you against acquiring your pup from an advertiser who lives a long distance from you and about whom you know nothing. Much of the information proferred concerning the pedigree of many litters which are for sale is the product of the fevered imagination of their breeder, and is very frequently tailored to suit the market for whatever is mostly in demand at any particular time. Some years back Deerhounds were popular so that just about every litter for sale purported to have a bit of Deerhound blood in it. Later on it became the turn of collies to turn up in the ancestry of anything which was a bit dicey and so it goes on. You may even fall prey to some dog dealer who is masquerading as a breeder and consequently has not the slightest clue as to the provenance of the wares which he has on offer.

BUYING A PUPPY

Having located what you consider to be a suitable breeder from whom to obtain your pup, you should get in touch with him or her and make arrangements to view the litter. Do not pay any attention to any of those strictures about 'No time wasters'. Your time is just as valuable as theirs and looking at the goods entails no obligation to purchase. Anyway, time wasted in not making a sale is far from being unproductive from a breeder's point of view for, in this way, he is able to meet all sorts of interesting people, as well as perhaps having his outlook broadened a bit.

At the same time as making an appointment to inspect the litter you should also make a point of asking to see both the dam and the sire. In normal circumstances there should be no difficulty about the bitch being present although viewing the sire may not be quite so straightforward. Again it helps a good deal should you know the owners of the parents. As has been the case thus far, do not accept too much at face value. Horse copers used to have a certain reputation, secondhand car dealers still have it and dog breeders who are not subject to the restrictions imposed upon pure bred breeders by the Kennel Club may sometimes fit in quite well with the two foregoing categories of trader. About the only sort of dog with which you can be fairly certain of getting that which you have paid for is the Greyhound, where the National Coursing Club allows very little in the way of loopholes due to its excellent system of recording. Whilst Kennel Club pedigrees are reasonably reliable, even they lack the rigid system of identification made mandatory by the NCC.

As an example I would just say that upon one occasion I was offered a lurcher pup and shown not only the dam, a registered Deerhound, but also what were described as the sire and dam's dam as well. I subsequently learnt that the only genuine member of the family, other than the pups, had been the mother of the litter. This little scam was tried on by someone whom I regard as a close friend and whom I would trust with my most treasured possession – but not in acquiring a lurcher!

You must be prepared for misinformation in every aspect of making your purchase, and this can happen even in the matter of age, where again strangers will sometimes tell you just about anything they think that you may wish to hear. Untruth apart, it is not always possible to obtain a puppy of what one may consider to be the ideal age. Difficulties of advertising and so on can lead to the litter being somewhat older than the age at which you would have wished to obtain a pup or for that matter, at which the breeder would wish to sell them for no one much relishes the idea of having too many hungry mouths to feed.

So what is the ideal age? In my own case I always try to get a pup at six weeks of age although you will probably find a good many breeders, particularly those more interested in the dogs which they breed than in the money which they receive for them, who will insist on a pup being eight weeks old before it goes. Anyway one should always endeavour to take delivery of one's young entry at as early an age as is possible because of the importance of socialising the pup. Should your breeder have a family of young children who are amongst the pups, playing with them and handling them a good deal, or should the litter be running in and out of the owner's house and receiving plenty of human attention, then I would not rate early age as such a major point. Should the youngster be of the right sort and suit you in every other way I would not think that three or even four months would be too great an age although in some circumstances, things like house training may be a problem.

Which puppy should you choose from the litter, always assuming that you get a choice. Sometimes (all to infrequent an occurrence, speaking as a breeder) they are all spoken for except one. No doubt you will receive a good deal of well meaning advice from acquaintances on this score and this will generally be to the tune of having the one which gets to the grub bowl first and bosses all the others. In actual fact, should you follow this precept, you will almost certainly find yourself with the most aggressive animal in the litter. This can frequently develop into a major problem in itself.

A rather better way to my mind is to quietly observe the litter for a while. If you are able to spot any obviously nervy specimens, write them off immediately. Handle the pups as much as you are able. They will not show much in the way of longdog characteristics at this stage but you may be able to see the one with the longest back. Tails are not a bad guide either, those with the longest ones often turning out to be the more 'houndy'. Look for good solid bone structure with those characteristic lumps around the foreleg; these grow out and at this stage denote future length of leg. Above all make sure that the pup is sound in wind and limb, not lame in any way and with a well formed jaw. Dentition is still at the stage of it having its milk teeth and so is not much of a guide but have a look in its mouth and see that all is well. Make sure by obvious means that it is neither deaf nor blind and it is just possible that you may have the right one.

The price which you should be prepared to pay is difficult to indicate in these days of inflation but, as with other commodities, prices are relative. On the whole, one should expect to pay less for a lurcher puppy than for a good one of authenticated pure breeding, although at the top end of the scale with breeders of David Hancock's standing I would not expect the figures to be very different. At the bottom end of the scale it is possible to find lurcher pups almost being given away. Price in itself, however, is by no means a ready means of assessing the true worth of the merchandise and many a good lurcher has, as a pup, been purchased for very little. All other things being satisfactory, and there being ample provenance as to parentage, I would be disinclined to let price assume over much importance in the matter and go for that which appeals to me rather than that which is *merely* expensive.

Other considerations may well come into it but I should be looking for my new lurcher pup at the beginning of the summer. Basic training is simpler at this time of the year and with luck your dog may be ready to enter to work in a small way before the end of the coming winter. Spring litters have a good deal in their favour over those bred during the colder months. But above all take your time and use all your senses in acquiring your lurcher pup. Unless it is something which is quite obviously well above average, do not purchase the first one which you are inclined to like for very little was ever done well in a hurry.

COLLECTING

When you go to pick up the youngster take some old material with you, an old jersey or two, or something of like nature. Failing that, a large towel will do, something which will wash easily. If you take your spouse or kids along, they will probably want to have the new puppy on their lap on the way home and puppy's tummies are not altogether reliable. You may be going on your own in which case still take some bedding of some kind for the same reason, and also so that the pup, which is leaving home and companions for the first time, may be that bit more comfortable.

On arrival at your destination pay for the pup, preferably in cash, and above all do not attempt to haggle on the price at this time. There are times for haggling and this is not one of them. Inquire when it had its last meal, what it had and what the situation is as regards worming and inoculations. It may have been wormed but is unlikely to have been inoculated unless it is 10 weeks old or more. Then it is tracks for home. Do not stop on the way but should it be imperative that you do so, do not let the puppy out of the car.

ARRIVING HOME

So you have arrived home. Take the puppy out into the garden, yard or what-have-you and give it a chance to do its business. There may be a good bit of sniffing and smelling about before it urinates or defecates but use your patience, a commodity of which you are going to require ample reserves during the next few weeks. Take the puppy inside, give it a drink of milk or water and a small meal after which take it outside again for a few minutes; the old waterworks can be quite active at this age. Its bed should have been ready for it and it may now be introduced to this. All will probably go well until bedtime after which be prepared for an unsettled night with a certain amount of howling and wailing. Warm quarters are a necessity and it helps to have something like a noisy clock ticking close by. After a night or two it should begin to settle down.

MAKING A START

The way in which you will make a start with the new entrant must depend to some extent upon whether you have acquired your puppy from another breeder or whether you have bred it yourself. In many ways matters will be simplified by your having bought in. You will have been able to obtain the animal at the age of eight weeks old or, should you have been fortunate, as soon as it has reached six weeks of age. There is no substitute for starting off at as early an age as is reasonable.

Should you have bred your own lurcher pup then you should make every effort to get it away from its fellows at around the age which I have indicated. If I am doing this myself I carry it out by the simple expedient of bringing the one which I have chosen into the house, leaving its fellows in their outside quarters. It now becomes a member of the family, its socialisation thereby being considerably reinforced. Henceforth it lives separately and is exercised separately from the other pups. This is a time consuming business but is worth every minute spent on it.

'But I haven't the time', I may hear you cry. How much time do you spend looking at television? How much time do you spend at the pub? How much time do you spend sleeping? What about that wonderful couple of hours after sunrise during the summer months? There is always time for something which you badly want to do.

The majority of lurcher owners do not breed their own but buy in from elsewhere. I have mentioned some of the considerations which are involved, earlier in this chapter.

Now we are at the moment of truth, that stage when you are about to fork out some of your hard earned cash for the privilege of taking on a responsibility which with a moderate amount of luck may be with you for the next 14 or 15 years for, barring accident, lurchers tend to be long-lived beasts.

A lurcher rescue puppy that made good.

LURCHER RESCUE

If for any reason you consider that it is absolutely necessary for you to have an adult dog rather than a puppy, I would suggest that you might give some thought to taking an animal from the Lurcher and Sighthound Welfare Association, secretary Mrs Fran Fisher, whose telephone number is 01494 773354 from whom, in my opinion, you are just as likely to get a useful lurcher as from rather more highly publicised sources, particularly bearing in mind the age old precept about 'self-praise being no recommendation'. This charity is doing an excellent job and by no means all the dogs which go through their hands are strays.

I would just add one caveat however, this being that this is a course which I would suggest to the experienced lurcher person rather than the novice. Good as many rescued dogs can be, there always remain a few which will be very unsatisfactory; for instance they may prove to be untrustworthy where livestock is concerned.

Rearing

FEEDING

You will have discussed with the breeder the matter of the sort of food which your puppy has been having and, unless this has consisted of something which you consider to be absolutely unsuitable, it will be as well to carry on with a similar diet for a few days in order to obviate the possibility of stomach upsets due to any sudden changes of food. It may have been having something such as tinned puppy food which although perfectly palatable and suitable in most other ways has little to recommend it by way of price. Making the change over gradually, should this be necessary, get it on to a meat and meal diet as soon as you can with milk once a day and an egg a couple of times a week. One sometimes hears that such foodstuffs are not suitable for dogs but they have stood the test of time and therefore are to be recommended on this score alone.

Should your pup be very young, say about six weeks of age, I would incline to giving it at least four meals a day but this can be cut down to three by the time that it is 10 weeks old and, unless it is extremely inconvenient, this regime should be adhered to until it is six months old when it can go on to two meals a day. I feed my adult dogs once a day which I (and they) find to be quite sufficient and they are following this dietary programme by the time they are a year old. Some people feed twice a day and really this is a matter best left to whatever suits you and your dog best.

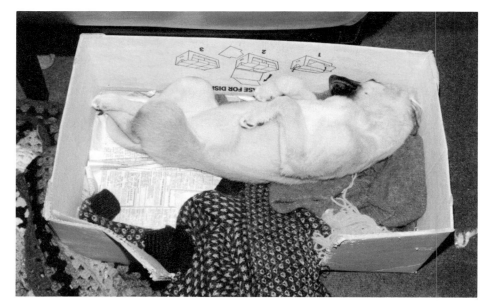

A cardboard box and an old jumper or blanket make an ideal basket for a puppy.

HOUSING AND SOCIALISING

I have gone into the subject of housing and feeding in the chapter on the management of adult dogs and whatever system you have decided to employ, now is the time to introduce the puppy to it. Whether it is quartered inside or outside your house, however, it should spend as much time as possible indoors amongst people, which should ideally include children. The more that they want to play with the puppy the better. Nevertheless it should not be removed from the confines of your own property until such time as its inoculations have been completed. These can be administered at the age of 10 weeks unless the puppy has left its mother at the age of six weeks in which case it can be earlier. The object of having a couple of weeks between weaning and inoculation is to provide an opportunity for the effects of the antibodies, which it will have been receiving in the bitch's milk, to wear off.

INOCULATION

The inoculation will be for Distemper, Hard Pad, Parvovirus and Leptospirosis and will consist of two injections, one as indicated two weeks after weaning and the other four weeks after the first one. These should give it protection against these four diseases, each of which is deadly, for the following 12 months when it should have a booster dose, this to be continued on an annual basis.

EXERCISE

As soon as the puppy has had its second injection it may be taken out in public, assuming that you have not wasted your time and opportunities during the time that it has been quarantined at home and have trained it to walk on a lead. Shortish strolls of a mile or so will do nicely for a start but you should get this up to longer distances as soon as you can. Walk it for about an hour every day and you should not be far wrong. Take it into town on market day, take it to the pub, or to the non-alcoholic equivalent if you are teetotal, and let it become used to other people and other dogs. It is all to the good if you should happen to have a cat and a few chickens and ideally a goat or sheep or two at this stage so that it can be stock trained with the minimum of effort. Although perhaps seeming to be a bit irksome at the time all this will save much trouble and effort at later stages in the animal's development.

WORMING

Whether or not the puppy is said to have been wormed prior to its leaving the breeder, worm it again as soon as it has settled in. Puppies are wormy little things and should be wormed on a regular basis once a month until they are six months of age. Keep an eye on its faeces whenever it passes them and always be prepared to worm as necessary. During this time round worms will be the worst nuisance but be prepared for tapeworm as well. Roundworms are not encountered to any great extent other than in pups and the pregnant bitch but tapeworms can be present in the adult dog at any time.

GROOMING

Unless they have a good deal of Bearded Collie blood in their makeup lurchers are not dogs which require much in the way of grooming but it is as well to give them a brush on a daily basis. Keep their claws trimmed to a reasonable length but make sure that you do not cut them too short and get into the quick when you do this. If they are getting plenty of road work on hard surfaces, however, little if any trimming will be found to be necessary.

BATHING

Should you wish to give your dog a bath, make sure that it does not get water in its ears or soap in its eyes. Personally I never bath my own dogs but they usually jump into the pond every day or so and have a dip. If you have a pond or lake available encourage your puppy to go into it and swim.

This is best done in the form of a game with other dogs and should never be attempted by throwing the dog bodily into the water. You may be told that lurchers cannot learn to swim. They can and are all the more useful by reason of being able to do so.

Elementary Training

The amount of training a lurcher requires differs, to some extent, according to the breeding of the dog and the use to which it is intended to put the animal. This may seem like the ultimate in simplistic statements and at face value perhaps it is. However, lurchers vary widely in many characteristics, even at times within the same breeding. Receptiveness to training can, and often does, vary within the same litter to a certain extent, although naturally by no means as much as it does between different strains and different crosses where the only thing that they have in common is longdog ancestry somewhere in the family tree. Training can be started from the time that the puppy is six weeks old with elementary retrieving, jumping, coming to name and whistle, sitting, down lessons and house training.

There exist certain types of lurcher which require very little in the way of training indeed for such dogs have their schooling bred into them so to speak; dogs of this sort are few and far between as might be expected. They are usually some sort of mongrel lurcher bred within a very close line in the same family, but whereas they must be what there owners want, they are by no means the sort of dog which we all require. I speak of those lurchers, not so common today as they were at one time, which are the ultimate in providers and fillers of the cooking pot, which are not particularly amenable to discipline and which work best by going their own sweet way. If you have never encountered one of these you have yet to meet your first true lurcher but this is not to say that this is the ideal running dog for today's lurcherman.

Dogs of this kind usually run to something between 20 and 23 inches in height and are brindle of coat. This general description fits a good many lurchers but when you meet the genuine article, should you be any sort of running dog expert, you will not take long to recognise it for what it is. Such a dog very frequently has another characteristic, which is not immediately apparent and is unlikely to manifest itself until the dog is worked; this is that many of them are weak of jaw. This is perhaps just as well when one considers the capacity in which such dogs are usually employed for these are the thieving lurchers, the pickers up of unconsidered trifles.

The first of these dogs that I ever met was the property of an old chap who lived in the venerable but at the time somewhat moribund

Lincolnshire town of Kirton-in-Lindsey. Perhaps I am being a bit unfair to the place but upon one occasion many years ago I found myself stranded there in a vehicle which defied all efforts to make it go in the middle of the town graveyard at two o'clock in the morning, which is the sort of situation which might cause anyone to have second thoughts about almost anywhere. It was said that the old man seldom left his house other than to visit the nearest pub and that the dog had never been known to leave or re-enter the premises except by means of the pantry window. It hunted on its own and quite independently of any human direction, going out whenever its owner decided to free it, always returning a bit later with something for the pot. Sometimes this would be a rabbit, sometimes a chicken, sometimes a pheasant or partridge or sometimes a duck, all of which would be retrieved to hand alive. Such quarry as hare or goose never figured on the menu for the lurcher was not capable of either holding creatures of this size or of carrying them home and was also probably not capable of killing a rabbit or a fowl but merely of carrying it back alive to its owner. This was the only dog of this kind which I had ever encountered at the time, 50 odd years ago, and I was not to meet with another until comparatively recently when I came across a strain of dogs which manifest much the same kind of character. These have been bred on what appears to be a haphazard system of inbreeding and are alleged to have originated from a strain kept by some, probably completely mythical, gypsy family. I am quite well acquainted with one of these animals and can confirm that it prefers to hunt on its own unaccompanied either by other dogs or its owner and indeed appears to prefer to live a solitary life in every way. It seems to have developed a predeliction for killing domestic fowl but also picks up rabbits in an effortless manner. It does not display the weakness of jaw which I would have expected but I am told that the person who breeds this line introduced bull terrier blood a few years ago to counter this defect. Unfortunately, whilst appearing to have had the desired effect, this has also caused the strain to become rather aggressive.

I was offered a pup from this breeding myself but declined since I prefer dogs with which I can become directly involved, both in their hunting activities and their everyday existence. However, as age and arthritis progress I may well regret my lack of foresight for such a dog could be worked from the confines of a Bath chair and would be capable of providing sustenance just as long as one's fingers remained supple enough to cope with the task of skinning a rabbit or plucking a fowl.

Generally speaking the least troublesome sort of lurcher to train is one which carries a fair amount of collie or gundog blood whilst those with a certain amount of terrier in them are less easy. It may be found though that many of these will drop into the right way of doing things with surprisingly little in the way of problems. Not only does the temperament of each dog have some bearing on the matter but so also has that of the individual owner. The fawning demeanour of some of the collie crosses may, for instance, irritate one person whilst the more boisterous outlook of some of the terrier bred dogs may be less acceptable to another. Oddly enough, although not all that oddly to those who have had much to do with gundogs, a few lurchers carrying labrador blood can be quite recalcitrant in some hands although fortunately this is not often the case.

I have stressed the matter of the owner's temperament because I believe this to be something of the utmost importance and an aspect of training which is too frequently not given sufficient consideration. A great many otherwise useful collie pups have been ruined in the course of preliminary schooling for the reason that they are apt to take any reprimand, sometimes of quite a mild nature, very much to heart. Terrier and gundog type lurchers being made of somewhat sterner stuff are less likely to suffer from having their feelings trampled upon in this way.

RETRIEVING

Retrieving is best taught with some small soft object (no, not the man next door) like a rolled up sock. Your pupil will probably show signs of wanting to carry this to its bed in the initial stages rather than to your hand. That makes things easier in a way. If it insists on doing this then sit in its bed when you throw the object. Encourage the pup to bring it back to you. Be lavish with praise and turn the whole thing into a game but do not forget that young things tire easily. At the first signs of boredom or lack of interest pack up immediately. Little and often should be the tenor of training at this stage. As you progress you should intercept the retrieval before the trainee reaches its bed and from there move on to encouraging it to bring the old sock or whatever in some other direction.

JUMPING

Jumping should also be initiated now by positioning a piece of 9″ board somewhere where the pup cannot avoid having to get over it. In a doorway or across a passage will do nicely, but do not forget to tell your nearest and dearest what is happening so that they do not measure their length over it (I am even throwing in a bit of marriage guidance counselling for good measure). As soon as it jumps over the obstacle with ease, substitute something a bit higher. This is all going to make things that bit easier at a later stage in training.

COMING BACK

Call the pup by its name as much as you can whenever feeding it and so on, but under no circumstances whatsoever admonish it by name. This is one of the commonest of mistakes made not only in training the young but also in the management of adult dogs. How often do you hear this sort of thing, 'Fido, you bad dog' preparatory to the dog getting a hard time in some shape or form. You do not want the dog to associate its name with something unpleasant like a telling off, for then it is going to be reluctant to come to you when you call it by name. If you want to call it by a name when it has committed some sin you will find the English language provides some quite suitable ones. Teach it to come to your whistle at an early stage as well.

HOUSE TRAINING

It is also never too early to commence house training a dog. Not by 'rubbing its nose in it' as is so frequently advocated but by taking it outside at the appropriate times; these being after feeding, at dawn, at midday and at dusk but above all when you see by its demeanour that it needs to be put out. This is easy enough to do if someone with a reasonably sharp eye is around most of the time. In those circumstances when the dog has to be left alone for long periods it is a good deal less easy. It is thus vital that when delivery is taken of a pup there should be someone about for the first week or two even if it means sacrificing some of your holidays for this purpose. Most of the Deerhound crosses which I breed are house trained by the time that they are eight weeks old. There is nothing phenomenal about this but simply a matter of constant vigilance. If you have to keep your dog in a kennel it should still be house trained and kennel trained as well for no one wants a dirty, smelly kennel. This is one of the curses amongst many others of buying in adult dogs. Bad habits which are simplicity itself to cure in a pup are often impossible to entirely overcome in a grown dog.

LEAD TRAINING

As soon as your pup has got over its inoculations and can go out its training proper can begin. It is never too early to start as long as it is carried out in a sensible and sympathetic way. Little and often remains the scheme of things and it should always be borne in mind that steady progress is usually preferable to anything meteoric. The first thing which must be done is to teach the pup to go on a lead, for in the first place it will be necessary to take it from home to whatever training ground may be available and in the second place a good deal of the elementary training will be on the lead. So it will now be necessary to consider the matter of leads and collars. Various ideas exist about these, the divergences of opinion remind one of the raging controversies which used to be conducted concerning the bitting of horses. In the case of a normal lurcher pup it would be as well to forget at the outset any ideas of using the choke chain collars which formed the anchor point of a popular television series, which apart from this aspect of dog training was otherwise quite good. Should you be unfortunate enough to have a dog which presents you with a serious problem of pulling against its lead then a choke chain collar has its uses, but most lurchers are comparatively light on the lead and, as pups at any rate, are unlikely to require remedial measures of this sort.

For most purposes of training young dogs, and for restraining adult ones, I have found the Turner-Richards type of slip lead ideal. This was devised by Peter Moxon for use with gundogs, in the training and handling of which he was second to none. It is lead and collar all in one and consists of a length of nylon or other cord with a fixed loop at one end and an adjustable sliding loop at the other. This necessitates there being a couple of splices which should be bound with leather, or at a pinch plastic tape, and a cord stop, also of leather, which can however be cunningly contrived with the aid of an ordinary tap washer. The lead is light, portable and fits comfortably into a pocket, or hangs round the trainer's neck when not in use. I usually make my own with the aid of a length of sash cord and the tongue of an old boot which, as any constructor of catapults will know, is the best source of reusable leather.

These leads would be well nigh perfect but for one failing, that they are not proof against the teeth of a lurcher, or longdog, should it decide to take a short cut to freedom. I had this forcefully brought home to me as I stood with my old Deerhound bitch, Fly, on a lead in a local pub whilst engrossed in conversation with of all people, the vicar. 'Invisible dog' wisecracked one of the local wags indicating the short length of cord in my hand, my dog was meanwhile engaged in helping itself to a plateful of sandwiches at the opposite end of the bar. The only answer to a lead biter, some of which are remarkably proficient at it, is a chain and an ordinary leather collar.

Having provided yourself with something suitable in the way of a lead the next thing to do is to accustom your pup to it. I am informed by those who go in for such dogs that the Bearded Collie based lurcher is exceedingly reluctant to accept either collar or lead. This by some strange form of reasoning is said to betray its Smithfield origins. I must confess that all other things being equal this purported difficulty would put me off bothering with such a dog, particularly when one considers how many other sorts of lurcher are available.

Most pups will accept a collar and lead without much trouble. The dog should be allowed to become accustomed to its collar by putting it on and leaving it to get used to it, always keeping an eye open at first just to make sure that it does not get a toe hung up in seeking to rid itself of the troublesome object. I am not an advocate, as are some trainers, of putting on the collar and attaching a lead to it, then letting the puppy go free. By doing this there is a distinct possibility of the animal becoming tangled in its lead and permanent lameness being the result. This is the last thing that anyone would want in a lurcher where it would not be merely tiresome, as in other dogs, but disastrous. As soon as it is used to the collar then give it a go on the lead. It is almost bound to rebel against this restraint at first and will pull against it and leap around a bit. Walk it around and it should soon settle down. The younger they are, the quicker they will be to accept the lead and once it has reached this stage and its inoculations are done it may be taken out and away from home so that serious training may commence.

SUITABLE LOCATION

You will probably have some suitable location in mind for your training sessions, but should you not have decided upon one then the best rule to follow is that the quieter it is the better. Should you not be able to find such a place then it will be necessary to get up early in the morning before anyone else is abroad, for peace and quiet is of the utmost importance. This is yet another plus in favour of summer pups for the sun rises in good time in May, June and July. Not many people are about to get in your way in the fields, and public open spaces are relatively uncluttered.

SOCIALISATION

Whilst some sort of isolated location, such as I have described, should be found for the training sessions, the continuing socialisation of the dog should not be neglected. It should be taken with you whenever possible into populated centres where there will be plenty of people, traffic and other dogs about. If you go to pubs, give those your custom which have no objection to taking a dog in there with you. Get your pup used to all these things and it will be far less likely to get into fights, bite people and be hysterical near traffic than it would otherwise have been.

BREAKING TO LIVESTOCK

Now is also the time to break it to livestock, probably the most important part of any lurcher's training. If you are fortunate enough to have your own sheep, cattle and poultry so much the better, but if not do your best to discover some friendly farmer who will not become neurotic when you introduce your pup to his stock. A puppy which is not much larger than a hen is far easier to train off livestock than is a grown dog, or even a half grown one. Take it amongst them and be ready to curb the slightest signs of vice of any kind, even if this amounts to no more than playful behaviour. What starts off as a game can swiftly become something more serious if warning signs are disregarded. If a dog ever becomes a sheep worrier, or a poultry killer, it will be found that this is an exceedingly difficult habit to break. Various cures have been suggested varying from fastening the dog up with an old tup to running a flock of sheep over it, but a confirmed stock worrier is very apt to remain a pest of this kind for the rest of its days, which very frequently will be found to be short. Should you be absolutely unable to obtain access to livestock then you should take your pup for walks where stock are present, keeping it on the lead of course. Take it close to the stock and as soon as it shows signs of too much interest in the animals, utter the word 'Sheep' in menacing tones, meanwhile giving a sharp tug on the lead. This is frequently quite enough to transmit the general idea to most dogs, but care should be taken particularly with collie blooded dogs whose instinct is to gather the stock, perhaps not leaving matters at that stage but taking a bite just to prove the point. Make no mistake about it; stock worrying or even stock chasing can prove to be an extremely expensive proceeding quite apart from attracting the general opprobrium of the righteous and the snide cracks of all your pals.

Should the dog still exhibit an unsatisfactory attitude towards livestock then try the effects of a check lead. A fairly long one of about 20 feet or so of strong cordage will do nicely. Again take the dog to the stock and when you are close enough to them, slip it off the short lead, having made doubly certain that the check lead is thoroughly secure both to the dog's collar and in your grip. Should it demonstrate any signs of wanting to have a go at the stock which, things being what they are, will usually consist of sheep, give it due warning in the way which I have described but, should it pay no attention to you, give it plenty of rope on the check lead and then pull it up with a jerk. I do not have much to do with breaking gundogs these days but in my youth this was the usual way in which gamekeepers dealt with a persistent runner in to rabbit, this being regarded as a major fault in a retriever. The dog should then be suitably admonished.

PUNISHMENT

This would seem to be an appropriate point at which to discuss the matter of corporal punishment. We have been told by those who purport to know all about the problem that our children should never be subjected to it. Any time now they will be taking the same sort of attitude concerning our dogs. I realise that I am treading on dangerous ground here and my own opinion on the matter, leaving aside, thank goodness, the subject of children, is that in the case of many dogs nothing more is ever required other than a sharp word. There remains however the type of offender to whom the only solution is a short, sharp lesson, however, striking them with anything must be your last resort. The best way of dealing with such dogs, in my experience, is to seize the animal by the scruff of its neck and give it a severe shaking, all the time looking it straight in the eye and letting it know in no uncertain tones what you think about its conduct. This is much the way in which its mother has dealt with it as a pup and a way which usually proves to be efficacious. However, there may just be an occasion upon which you are forced to put your point even more forcibly and stock chasing is one such time.

If the dog has to be beaten, never hit it with your hand for this will make it handshy. By the same token never strike it with a lead. The only instrument for use in such a case is a thin whippy stick, preferably cut from the nearest hedgerow and discarded at the end of the proceedings. I can only add that of my present three dogs I have had to lay violent hands on only one of them, and that but once in the course of over 10 years.

SIT

Having, I hope, covered the preliminaries we can now move onto the basic commands. The first, and to my mind, the foremost thing which it must be taught is to go down when required to do so. This is the basic command for, once this has been mastered, the dog is henceforward under control. The ability to put it down and keep it down should give you absolute control of practically any situation which is likely to develop.

Most books on the subject of dogs will tell you that in order to teach a dog to sit it should be put into the required posture by means of gently pushing down its hindquarters. Most dogs will resist this pressure by wriggling

A six month old puppy sitting and staying on command.

their backsides about in the manner of some hula hula dancer rather than doing what is required of them. There is one easy answer to it all. Simply grasp the dog between finger and thumb above its loin, just forward of its hips, and squeeze. The dog will then obligingly sit down. It should of course be on a lead when you are carrying this out and with the other hand you should hold its head up, otherwise it may just roll over on to its back, which whilst no doubt to the dog's mind engaging, is not what you were after.

Whilst doing this you should give the command 'Sit'. This should have mastered the first part of the operation from where it is just a matter of constant repetition. Once again the key to success is frequent training sessions of short duration.

LIE DOWN

Once the pup begins to understand what you mean when you tell it to sit you may progress to the next stage which is to get it to lie down on command. This is achieved by getting it to sit and then giving the necessary order 'Down' and taking it by its front legs, draw these forward from under it. Once again it is not much use at this stage to try pushing the dog's front end down as is sometimes advised. If you try to do it this way this will usually be followed by resistance and a struggle. Far easier to carry it out as I recommend. Again this exercise must be the subject of constant, but I hope not too monotonous, repetition. The scheme of training should remain little and often and training sessions should never be prolonged to the point of boredom, either for you or the dog, and should preferably be carried out at least three times a day. Since most people have to earn a bit of money to keep at any rate the dog in luxury, they will not be able to put in more than two training periods a day but this should be regarded as the absolute minimum. As the opportunity presents itself, for instance at weekends, try to put in more training time for the end result is going to be well worth having. Above all, remember that nothing goes perfectly all the time and so **never allow yourself to become despondent**.

STAY

Having achieved success to this point now comes what some trainers regard as the severest test of all, this is to train the dog to stay where it has been put. It is not an easy lesson to put over but nonetheless is about the most valuable one that can be taught to a lurcher.

There are some dogs which never seem able to manage to stay when told to do so, but the majority will get hold of the idea, some of course faster than others. Success is usually brought about by means of endless patience and persistence, but once achieved is well worth all the hard work. No attempt to teach the stay should be made until the dog is going down satisfactorily on the command 'Down'. As I have mentioned previously this is the basic command and with it the dog may be anchored

It is essential for a working dog to have some form of obedience. You must at least be able to make it lie and stay in one position until told to move.

where it is, so controlling it whenever necessary, even perhaps saving it's life on certain occasions. For this piece of schooling it is necessary to take your pupil to some location where you will be unlikely to find anything at all in the way of disturbance. Put the dog to the 'Down' without the lead, stand with it for a short time, and then start to back away from it giving the command 'Stay'. Hold up your hand in the same way as did the old time policeman when he wished to halt the traffic, and back away a step at a time. The dog will almost certainly attempt to get up and follow you but any signs of this must be severely nipped in the bud. After a few attempts you will probably be able to retreat a few steps before it tries to rise but whenever it does so make sure that you put it back on exactly the same spot where you started off and then have another go. It should eventually get the message and you will be able to back away for some 20 or so yards. At this stage, do not call the dog to you. Go back to it, put it on the lead, make much of it, take it a short distance away and repeat the exercise. Repeat this once more and pack up for the day. You have earned a rest.

From this stage it is a matter of constant repetition until something like perfection is attained. Now another hurdle confronts you and this is to repeat the exercise yet again, but this time turn your back on the dog as you walk away from it. It will probably seize the opportunity, now that you are no longer regarding it with your hypnotic eye, to tag on behind you or maybe just to get up and come forward a few steps. As before put it back in exactly the same place that you had left it. In all fairness it must be said that this stage of the proceedings rarely takes as long as the first one, which must be regarded as the crucial part of the business. At any time during this phase of training, and even after it when the dog appears to have thoroughly learned the lesson, it may still try creeping forward on its belly with a sort of 'this does not count' expression on its face. Curb this immediately and put it back to station.

Yet another milestone has been passed. It is now time to put the dog into the stay position and to go away out of sight somewhere, adopting the same method of training as previously. There will be plenty of setbacks at all these stages but keep it uppermost in your mind that patience and perseverance took a snail to Jerusalem. You may wind up by thinking that the snail had a pretty easy time of it compared with your own experiences, or at least have a certain amount of fellow feeling for the gastropod.

It is now time to reinforce your early lessons at the puppyhood stage of getting the dog to come to call. A fairly simple matter after the previous training, but one which is all too often rather skimped for the reason that it appears to be elementary. If the dog is sitting, going down and staying on command by now, it will be all the easier to ensure that it responds to call promptly. Leaving it a little way off at the stay, call it to you by name. Praise it and make much of it. When it is doing this automatically, teach it to come to your whistle. You will have come quite a long way by now. Keep up the training by constant reinforcement. No dog remains trained if it is not kept constantly up to the mark. Be lavish in praise and correct faults firmly but never harshly.

Further Training

If you have managed to train your dog to the standard suggested in the first part of this chapter you will be able to pride yourself on having something which is not all that common, a trained dog. From here you can go on so that you not only have a trained dog but also a well trained lurcher, which is even more of a rarity. It is not often that one encounters what could be regarded as an all round lurcher in these days of specialisation. In dogs as in people it is often a case of less and less knowing more and more or, should you cynically wish to put it the other way, more and more knowing less and less.

Even within the narrow confines of specialisation, however, it is quite common to find a dog which is other than perfect at doing its job. The vast majority of lurchers today hunt on the lamp but of all these one wonders just how many can be classed as first class retrievers. Of those which are taken out with ferrets, how many will mark sensibly, or even remain where they have been stationed?

Before commencing any form of advanced training it is absolutely vital that your dog should be able to follow all the elementary commands without fault or hesitation. Should it not measure up to this standard, why not take it along to obedience classes? There is nothing infra dig about this, most of the trainers are excellent at their jobs and you will also be able to get a bit of insight into the problems which other people encounter.

Let us assume that the dog is behaving satisfactorily in every way; that it will sit, lie down, stay where put and will come when called. Where do we go from here? Well first we go a bit further with some of the lessons already taught. This may sound a bit of a bore but it will be considerably less tedious than were the early schooling sessions. Not only will the dog be swifter to respond but also you will be better able to see where you are going and there will be a good deal more purpose in your activities.

HAND SIGNALS

Now is the time to improve upon dropping the dog into sitting and lying down positions and ensuring that it stays there even when it is at a distance from you. It should now be taught to carry out these movements to manual signs. This is accomplished by using a hand signal whenever a command is given by voice, and should initially be performed on the lead. From there it is a matter of practising the same exercises at ever increasing distances, increasing these by quite small amounts, say 25 yards at a time. The dog may now also be introduced to the so called 'soundless' dog whistle. This is not exactly what the name implies but is simply a whistle which is tuned to a very high pitch, one which although audible to everyone other than those who are hard of hearing is still not too obvious. They have the added advantage of possessing a range considerably in excess of any whistle which could be produced by human means. The dog is trained to come to the high frequency whistle in the same way that it has been taught to come to its name. Start close at hand and increase distances as your pup becomes more proficient. It is also advisable to teach the dog to come to a snap of the fingers and a click of the tongue. When working it fairly close these are the best ways of summoning it and are far less likely to disturb quarry, or anything else, than other methods. Tongue clicking is particularly useful in this respect. In the old days of poaching with long nets this was the usual way of communication between those taking part and can, therefore, be said to have withstood the test of time.

REINFORCING THE CALL

From time to time one encounters dogs which will not come when called and one way of overcoming this is to crouch down when calling the beast. The dog's natural curiosity will frequently cause it to approach this strange looking object, and it may be introduced to the proper way of doing things by this method.

FURTHER RETRIEVING

All lurchers should retrieve to hand and the last thing that anyone would want to do when lamping rabbits is to have to go out and pick up. If you have entered into plenty of retrieving games from an early age it is quite likely that your lurcher will be inclined to retrieve naturally. Most of my Deerhound hybrids will do this and, according to some authorities on the subject, these are not regarded as the easiest dogs in the world to school. I am perhaps fortunate in having an old and steady retriever to help put them into the way of it but, even without this sort of help, retrieving is something which should come naturally, provided the dog is introduced to it as a game at an early age. Indeed some dogs are persistent retrievers to the point of being a nuisance by bringing you all manner of strange objects, much in the same way that there are others who are persistent herders, rounding up everything from fowls to small children. Whilst the general rule with training of any kind is to school the puppy on its own, well away from people and above all, other dogs, there are times when the presence of another dog can be of assistance and one of these occasions is

If you perfect the retrieving part of the dog's training you will find that when it starts catching rabbits it will instinctively bring them back to you.

the case of the reluctant retriever. In this instance, of course, the other dog should ideally be one which is accomplished in this activity.

Once your pupil is successfully retrieving a small and portable object try it with something a bit bigger, working up to a dummy about the weight of a hare. The progression must always be gradual and the dog should never be presented with anything which is going to cause it any difficulty. You will find if treated as a game the dog will soon start to retrieve anything you throw out for it, even a metal object. From here it is a short step to placing a dummy some distance away and sending the dog over to fetch it. If you perfect this part of the dog's training you will find that when it starts catching rabbits it will instinctively bring them back to you. But be prepared for the occasional rebellion in the early days with live game, do not get angry with the young dog, just persevere with the training and all will come right as it matures.

QUARTERING

Quartering is often carried out instinctively by the working dog, but in some cases has to be taught. If your dog does not range freely it may be encouraged to do so by the use of food. In this case by throwing out Shapes, or other small biscuits, on alternate sides as you walk across a field. Once the animal finds some form of quarry whilst quartering in this way it will not be slow to put two and two together and start to run out naturally. I prefer to teach a pup to quarter before walking to heel since, should one do things the other way about, it is sometimes more difficult to induce them to leave your side.

HEEL

Heel training should be taught on the lead. Walk the dog along beside you on a fairly short lead and whenever it decides to leave you, give a good sharp tug on the lead, one which will have some effect on it. Anything in the nature of a steady pull should be avoided and the dog must be made fully aware that it is being corrected. At the same time as you do this utter the word 'Heel'. Take it around on a lead in this way as frequently as is possible. After a few weeks of this regime dispense with the lead and again with the command 'Heel' walk along with the dog in the same position as it would have been in had you been using a lead. An easy way to encourage the dog in this is to have a piece of biscuit in your hand. Some sort of a light switch, the sort that you cut out of the hedgerow is ideal, should also be carried and any attempt by the dog to leave its proper position should be corrected with a light tap. As in all other branches of training, correct incipient faults at the outset before they become too much of a problem. Do not abandon the lead altogether but continue heel training on it whenever you are able. Of course always keep it on a lead when anywhere near traffic no matter how well it walks at heel.

FURTHER JUMPING

You will have taught the pup the rudiments of jumping as described in the section on elementary training. It should now be ready for the real thing. Whenever you take it out for a walk make this as much of an obstacle course for the animal as you can. Encourage it to jump over obstacles, to creep through holes in hedges and to walk over narrow planks. Far too many lurchers and longdogs are not capable of dealing with a simple

Kevin Beaumont's Lurcher bitch, Abbey, clears a six bar gate with ease.

obstacle when they are confronted with one and it is both tiring and embarassing to have to lift them over everything that you come to.

When teaching a dog to jump, just as when you are training it to do anything else, remember always to progress by means of small doses but at the same time, ever increasing small doses. Never take things to the point of either fatigue or even of plain boredom. At the slightest signs of disinterest pack up whatever you are doing there and then. If carrying on with the training sessions switch to some other activity.

If you have carried on with elementary jumping training, and assuming that you are not having to spend all your time in the local hospital visiting those various members of your family and friends who have fallen over your cunningly contrived obstacle course, your lurcher should by now have first learned to scramble over and then to leap over the various bits and pieces with which you have littered its path. Find something a bit higher now and if such does not seem to exist, make up hurdles and so on in the paths which you frequent. Should courting couples, whilst fondly gazing into one another's eyes, trip over them in the dark it will make life all that bit more interesting for them, something which they can look back upon in their future lives of connubial bliss.

On approaching any sort of obstacle put your dog into the 'Sit' or the 'Down' position, give it the command to stay, climb over the fence or whatever it happens to be, go on for 20 or so yards and then call the dog. The odds are that the creature will be so keen to get to you that it will put on a good bit of speed so that it will completely clear its fence rather than crawl over it. This is the thing to encourage.

Carry on in this way with your dog going clean over the top of whatever stands in his path and before long you will be ready to tackle the modern farm fence. This usually consists of netting with three rows of barbed wire on top. This is where you have to be careful for it is only too easy for a young dog which is jumping well to go at such a fence, not see the barbed wire and get hung up on top. Should this ever happen, get there as fast as you can and lifting him up clear of the wire, get him right away from it. Injury apart, becoming hung up on wire can put a dog off jumping such fences altogether. So do not let it happen.

In order to train your dog to clear such obstacles take off your coat and wrap it over the top strand of wire, so that in the first place he can see what he is going over and in the second will not damage himself even if he does hit it. It is at this stage that you will appreciate why your dog has been trained to go over an obstacle leaving a fair amount of daylight between itself and the fence, or whatever it happens to be. Fence crawlers stand an exceedingly good chance of failure and serious injury.

From here you may go on, or perhaps I should say up. The times when you are confronted with an eight foot wall may be few and far between; but there are always agility competitions to be entered. You might even wish to cut a dash by putting your lurcher over the top of a bus, as has said to have been accomplished by some of our better known extroverts.

GOING INTO COVER

In the course of exercising your dog you will probably pass some bits of rough scrub, bramble patches and the like. Encourage your dog to get into these and hunt around. Edible training again comes into the picture; throw bits of biscuit into such cover and it is quite likely that your lurcher

John Bayles stands by while Jack, his Whippet/Collie cross, works the cover.

will go in after them. I would not want to go any further than to say that this may be quite likely since there are some lurchers which will never go into cover. This does not seem to have anything to do with what sort of a coat the dog might have. I have known plenty of thin skinned little Whippets which will go into cover like terriers and rough coated dogs that do not want to have anything to do with it.

There are two schools of thought regarding whether or not lurchers should go into cover. Some owners like them to go in and hunt out in the same manner as a Spaniel or a terrier, but there are others who prefer their dogs to stay outside the rough so as to be ready to take off and catch anything which emerges, bolting the quarry by means either of terriers or their own bush beating activities. There is something to be said for each of these schools of thought and in the end I think it just comes down to what sort of country you are hunting. If cover should be sparse then by all means get into it with your own hob nailed boots but where it is more or less continuous and the quarry flits from patch to patch it will probably be as well if your dog will get in amongst it.

In any case I would think twice before bolting your game from cover with the assistance of terriers. I know that bushing is established practice in a good many places but I would still be hesistant to recommend it. In my experience more running dogs have been ruined this way than by any other. Terriers being what they are, fairly aggressive characters, will dispute a catch which can either put the gentler dispositioned lurchers right off hunting or may cause them to develop some very tiresome and undesirable habits such as consuming their catch. On the other hand and particularly in the case of longdogs, it is possible to wind up with a dead terrier.

TRAINING TO THE GUN

It may be that you wish your lurcher to work to a gun. There is no reason at all why it should not do so and a lurcher which has been trained to the gun can be, and sometimes is, the equal of a pure bred Spaniel or retriever. If you have come with me as far as this your dog will already be retrieving, flushing game and dropping when required to do so, so you only need to train it to drop to shot just as it is already doing to verbal and manual commands. It will, however, be necessary to condition the dog to gunfire and this is quite simply done. Do not be tempted to expose it to the sound of a full charge going off at first, or it will probably become gunshy. Like mighty oaks which 'from tiny acorns grow', it is a matter of starting off from small beginnings and working up to bigger things. Start the dog off by discharging an airgun maybe nine or ten yards away from it. The time to do this is when it is feeding so that part of its mind is fixed on other and more pleasurable matters. Once it becomes used to this get a bit closer to it when you let the airgun off, and keep on getting nearer and nearer until after quite a short time you will be able to discharge the weapon within a foot or two of it without its taking notice. Then starting off in exactly the same manner go through the same rigmarole using a starting pistol. Next do it with .410 and keep on in this way until it is capable of standing the blast of the full bore with equanimity.

Having reached this stage, or maybe before this depending upon how enterprising your dog is, it will be time to enter him or her to quarry.

— 7 —
Management of the Adult Lurcher

It is an old saying that half the breeding goes in at the trencher and this still holds as true today as it did when the saying was first coined. There is a ready answer to feeding lurchers, which has also stood the test of time, and this is meat. However, as everyone will be well aware, there is meat and meat where the feeding of any carnivore, including the human kind, is concerned.

One thing has altered over the years, though, and that is the cost of meat for dog feeding which has increased astronomically so that the lurcher owner now needs to be as careful a shopper as the most economically minded housewife. A few short decades ago there was plenty of horsemeat to be had at reasonable prices and butchers' and slaughterhouse waste could frequently be had for the asking. This is no longer so.

TINNED FOOD

If you feed your dogs on any sort of tinned stuff you will be paying a fairly high price for it. Take out the gelatinised water content of a tin of dog food and you will discover that the remaining meat becomes very expensive. You may also discover that your canine charges are tending to scour a bit; this is the effect of an overabundance of water on the system. Mind you, all dogs seem to like tinned food and thrive on it and there is one time at which I would always feed it, which is when weaning a litter of pups, when tinned puppy food is an invaluable commodity. Tinned food needs to be fed in conjunction with a biscuit mixer, further adding to the cost.

It is a convenient way of feeding when one is away from home with a dog since it may be fed straight from the can, and, moreover, is in no way offensive to handle or to carry. In this respect it very definitely scores when compared with say sheep paunches or tripe with which I would not desire to share the interior of a small car for long on a hot day.

SHEEP PAUNCH

Sheep paunch is about the messiest and smelliest sort of meat which you can feed to your dog. At the same time it is nutritious and well accepted by lurchers, just as it is by Didicais who are likewise very partial to a dish of sheep stomachs, suitably blanched and cooked in their case of course. This portion of the ovine digestive tract as well as serving as a container for haggis was also used in Mau Mau oathing ceremonies and so it may be seen to be a pretty popular sort of commodity with all manner of applications. This is not the reason why it is currently in short supply, however, this being due to an entirely different and less interesting cause, in fact a dead boring one, to wit E.E.C. Food (Health and Hygiene) Regulations which have interfered with the running of slaughterhouses and abattoires in much the same way that such extra-national legislation interferes with everything else in our lives. Paunch and tripe, like tinned food, need to be accompanied by a biscuit mixer.

TRIPE

The same considerations apply to the supply of beast paunches (tripe), although these are obtainable from pet food dealers once they have been suitably sterilised according to the whims of our lords and masters in Brussels. For some reason or other, the basis of which should not be too difficult to divine, this sterilisation process always seems to involve the addition of fair quantities of water to the product so that when it has been defrosted one is not left with quite the same weight of meat as one had perhaps budgeted for. Nevertheless, this still represents a perfectly natural dog food at a price which, though inflated by aqueous addition, is not too exhorbitant.

COMPLETE FOODS

As a result of the expenses involved in meat feeding, more and more dog owners are turning to the dried dog foods such as Wilsons, Vitalin,

Nubbliedog and so on. These have an animal protein content and are prepared on a balanced basis and are complete feeds in themselves. I have fed my own dogs on these, sometimes for quite long periods, and have never noticed any falling off in condition or performance, and they never seem to upset the canine digestive system in any way. Having said that, one cannot help noticing that dogs do not swallow such food down as they would a dish of smelly offal and tend to adopt irregular feeding patterns. I suppose we would do the same ourselves should we be compelled to exist on an exclusive diet of breakfast cereal.

HOW MUCH TO FEED

How much to feed? My rule as far as any working dog is concerned is to feed as much as it will eat. Under this sort of regime many breeds will swiftly become obese, but this seldom occurs with the lurcher. In those cases when your lurcher is a singleton there may be difficulty in getting it to feed at all, which you would not encounter even if you had so much as a cat to represent some sort of challenge. The answer, where no form of rivalry for food exists and a dog starts to be a bit pernickety about its rations, is to starve it for a day or two at a time if necessary. You have to be fairly hard hearted about this sometimes but the result is usually that the dog, which has previously been picking away at its victuals, will then ravenously consume anything put before it. I well remember someone with an Afghan Hound getting to the stage where the thing would turn its aristocratic nose up at anything other than the best fillet steak. I have not the slightest doubt that had the creature been subjected to a short, sharp course of starvation it would have fallen upon fortnight old paunch with gusto.

BONES

It is a good idea to give your dog a regular bone, not one that will splinter but something a good deal heftier, such as a marrow bone, that will provide hours of happy gnawing. Not only will this provide him with more pleasure but it will help to keep his teeth clean and healthy.

HOUSING

Having provided for the dog's inner wellbeing, there is its general comfort to be considered. Unless it is strictly necessary to do otherwise, the best place for any dog is inside its owner's home. Lurchers, in my opinion, are best kept as a single dog and the constant company of other dogs, depending upon breed and disposition, can prove to be a very positive drawback where a lurcher is concerned. If you have a single lurcher, it should not prove too difficult to arrange its accommodation in some part of your house. The advantages are manifold; such an animal will develop an empathy with its owner that it would never do if confined to a kennel, even one which is alongside the house. Have it as close to you as you are able, in your bedroom for preference.

If you have never done this before you will be quite surprised by the difference in the dog's general attitude and how much easier it is to train. It will develop a completely different outlook from that of dogs which are kennelled outside. There is also the matter of security to be considered. This is a two way transaction for not only will your dog be on hand to deter intruders but also, in these days of lurcher thefts, will stand much less chance of being stolen.

Just about the most unsuitable site is a kennel at the far end of the garden. Should you get away with not having the dog or dogs stolen, there is the problem of tiresome individuals, frequently juveniles whose idea of having a bit of fun is to go along and tease someone else's dog. The further away from the house your dog is kennelled the less attention it is likely to get. The extreme case is when the dog is only taken out for a hunting trip and the owner then wonders why he has such a poor rapport with the dog and their efforts produce so little in the way of results. If it is absolutely necessary to kennel your dog outside, then have it somewhere close to the house.

As to the accommodation itself, there is some very good sectional housing (referred to by our local Mrs Malaprop as 'sexual' housing) to be had, but this does tend to become a bit expensive and if anyone is anything of a handyman he can soon knock up something suitable either in timber or in masonry. Floors should be of concrete so that they can be cleansed without too much difficulty. Such floors do tend to be rather cold and it is not a bad idea to provide some sort of insulation under them. Empty bottles are quite useful for this as are old egg containers. Where these are incorporated, a bit of air space is provided which makes conditions a good deal more comfortable for your hound.

If you are building in brick or stone, do not forget the damp proof course. This is just as essential in any form of animal housing as it is in your house. A bench should also be built into the structure to provide a place for the dog's bed off the floor well out of draughts. Make it large enough, though. The best way of ensuring that this is so, is to work out the size that you will require and then double it. As anyone knows, a bed that is too narrow or too short is both uncomfortable and irritating. Carried to its ultimate, accommodation of this kind provided the medieval 'Little-Ease' which was an extremely constricted form of cell in which people confined their enemies when they captured them. It was so constructed that the victim could neither lie down, sit up, nor stand. In places like Carrickfergus Castle an added refinement was added, the dungeon being so sited that the sea washed into it at high tide. Think about such things when erecting any form of accommodation for animals, for this is the sort of thing that people did to their worst enemies. So do not do it to man's best friend.

Last but not least, provide some form of roofing which is not going to overheat in the summer. Corrugated iron is just about the worst material for doing this but all unceilinged housing can warm up a bit on a hot summer's day. There should be adequate ventilation of course and some form of outside yard so that the dog can stretch its legs from time to time.

How many should be kennelled together? This is a moot point and I would immediately give the answer that one dog per kennel is ideal. At the same time I realise that this is not always possible in which case I would say that as long as both dogs are lurchers, then there may be a fair chance that they will get on together. On no account ever kennel a terrier with a lurcher for this is a fair recipe for a dog fight and very likely a dead terrier. Although it is not within the ambit of this book I would mention that two terriers housed together will almost certainly be a basis of trouble although, depending on the terriers, you just may be able to get away with it. Three terriers kennelled together are a certain step on the road to disaster for two will gang up on one with almost always fatal results for the odd one out. By the same token I would certainly never put three lurchers together for, although lurchers do not possess the same sort of jealous disposition as do terriers, the same problem of two ganging up on one will almost certainly be encountered. Some dogs manage to get on together; others will never do so. Yet another reason, should you be a lurcherman, for sticking to one dog and one dog only.

EXERCISE

The majority of lurchers will benefit from being walked five miles or so every day. Ideally this should be partly over hard surfaces and there should also be an opportunity for them to stretch their limbs and have a gallop. However, even if this is not always possible I would say that an adult lurcher should be exercised for at least 45 minutes every day.

GROOMING

Most lurchers are either smooth or broken coated, long haired Bearded Collie types being less common. Some owners seldom groom their dogs and this becomes abundantly obvious when one is judging at a lurcher show by reason of one's hands becoming soiled in a remarkably short time merely by running them over some of the various dogs which are shown. The amount of grooming which a dog should receive must depend to a very great extent upon length of coat, the longer haired sorts obviously needing more in this way than do dogs with short and broken coats. Nevertheless even short haired dogs should be brushed at least once a day. Not only will this ensure that the dog becomes used to being groomed but it will also provide an opportunity for the owner to notice any minor cuts and abrasions or other injuries which might have otherwise passed unnoticed.

Again some owners bath their dogs frequently whilst others seldom if ever afford them this privilege. As far as I am concerned I bath my dogs only when I consider that they need it, which is fairly seldom, but then I have the benefit of several large ponds nearby and they not infrequently have a dip in one or other of these. I realise that the majority of lurcher owners are not so well situated as this but I would recommend that they put their dogs in the tub only when they need it, for instance if they are dirty or if they need some sort of medicinal bath as a remedy for insect infestation or other skin troubles.

AILMENTS

Most lurchers, being in reality some sort of canine mongrel, albeit with a strong dash of the longdog in their makeup, have remarkably strong constitutions. They should, of course, be given the normal routine inoculations against distemper, hardpad, parvo and leptospirosis as soon as they are weaned and annually thereafter and should be wormed from time to time, preferably at spring and again at the onset of winter. Just as long as the routine safeguards are regularly carried out there is not much that lurchers are prone to suffer from. Unlike many darlings of the Kennel Club and Crufts, lurchers are unlikely to suffer from hip dysplasia and retinal detachment and other complaints of this nature.

The main health problems that occur with running dogs are those of injury, and in this respect they are much more likely than other sorts of dog to become casualties. The main reason for this is, of course, their superior speed and acceleration. Quite apart from injury due to collision with inanimate objects, such as fences and trees whilst proceeding at high speed, there are also a good many broken bones, strains and dislocation of joints by reason of the sheer power of such dogs. Basically put a foot wrong and something has to go.

Fortunately by dint of their superior constitutions, running dogs of all kinds are usually able to recover from these sort of mechanical complaints without too much trouble. Their bones knit well and their flesh and ligaments heal rapidly. However, injuries should not be left untreated and, in the case of severe problems like breakages, major cuts, abrasions and dislocations, you should waste no time getting the patient to the nearest veterinary surgeon.

For minor complaints, old fashioned remedies like Green Oils are hard to beat. These promote healing without giving rise to tiresome resistances and allergies as some of the modern wonder drugs are apt to do. Friar's

Balsam is another excellent old fashioned remedy which does not seem to have been surpassed by any of its modern equivalents. For the rapid healing of cut pads and so on which defy all efforts to stitch them, Friar's Balsam frequently proves to be a sovereign cure.

As a lurcher owner it is no bad thing to become versed as soon as you can in the elementary stitching up of wounds. Where dogs are concerned, it is not a case of a stitch in time saving nine but of a stitch in time perhaps saving your dog's life. To stitch a cut is not a difficult process to learn and some quite horrendous wounds particularly of muscles, which seem to burst asunder in quite a spectacular fashion, are rapidly brought under control with the prompt use of a needle and a length of surgical suture.

On the whole, whenever there is anything amiss with your lurcher, no time should be wasted in getting it along to your vet. Personally, I am a bit choosy about all my professional advisers and amongst these I include my veterinary surgeon. A good one with the correct attitude towards working dogs is a pearl beyond price. Take heed of his every word and do not begrudge what it costs (always within reason of course). Speaking very generally, I always seem to get the best advice and treatment for my animals from those who cater for all livestock including large ones, horse and cow vets as they used to be called. At risk of offending them, I would say that those practitioners with what are known as small animal practices are not for me, excellent as they undoubtedly are in dealing with pet dogs and cats. If you can find a vet who looks after Greyhounds, either in training establishments or at your local Greyhound track, he or she will usually be the sort of person that will be of some use to you.

When a dog suffers any sort of injury, other than one of the most minor character, there is one unpleasant and fairly rapid killer and that is shock. If your dog has any sort of accident do make sure beyond any sort of doubt that it is kept warm. Wrap it up in blankets, your coat, your jersey, your shirt, your undervest, if you wear one, and make sure that it loses the absolute minimum of body heat. Make sure that it has plenty to drink in the way of water or milk and, although alcohol is not recommended for the dog, a swift stiff dram might do you a power of good at such a time.

Various ailments will no doubt crop up occasionally and since it is as well to know something about these here are some of them, set for easy reference, in alphabetical order.

Abscesses
These may occur in any part of the body and contain pus. They arise from various causes through the introduction of dirt organisms. Hot fomentations and hot poultices will usually bring the abscess to a head when it will burst but it may sometimes have to be lanced and the dog treated with antibiotics.

Anaemia
Deficiency of red corpuscles in the blood. Can be due to malnutrition or repeated haemorrhages. Can sometimes be caused by worm infestation. Linings of eyelids, gums and mouth become pale and there is loss of energy. Treated by removal of cause and feeding with raw and underdone meat. Iron injections will help.

Anal Glands
The dog drags its hindquarters along the ground, 'sledging', licks the anus and tucks its tail in. The cause is frequently diagnosed (wrongly) as worms and the dog is dosed accordingly with unsatisfying results. Two glands lying on either side of the anus need to be squeezed out and then wiped with a piece of cotton wool soaked in a boracic solution. Some dogs require this treatment every few weeks.

Bites
A punctured wound caused by another animal, in the case of lurchers usually a fox. Cut away surrounding hair and syringe the wound with warm water and disinfectant (TCP is useful in this respect) to prevent wound healing from the top. Treat with green oils or Friar's Balsam. If wound is serious call the vet.

Breath, Bad
May be due to bad teeth or worm infestation. Remove the cause in whichever case.

Choking
Dogs may sometimes choke on a bone. This can sometimes be pulled out or pushed down using the fingers. If this fails give the dog some large pieces of meat to swallow in order to force the bone on. Should this not dislodge it consult the vet who will use forceps.

Collapse
May arise from accident. Lay the dog on its *right* side and ensure that it is kept warm. Summon the vet.

Constipation
Usually caused by unsuitable diet. Feed roughage. A feed of raw liver often helps.

Cuts
A fairly common injury in lurchers and frequently caused by running into barbed wire. Bathe with warm water containing disinfectant and apply green oils or Friar's Balsam if the cut is not a deep one. In the case of more

serious cuts, stitching may be necessary and, unless you are able to do this yourself with complete confidence, the services of the vet will have to be engaged without delay. Cuts in the foot where it is not possible to stitch should be treated with Friar's Balsam. After this has been copiously applied it should be bandaged over if possible and left to heal.

Diarrhoea

Give a desertspoonful of castor oil and starve for 12 hours after which the dog may be given a gruel of arrowroot and milk. If this does not effect a cure consult the vet as there will probably be an internal infection of some kind.

Distemper

Inoculate after weaning and regularly thereafter, also known as hard pad.

Eczema

Usually caused by an allergy, some strains of lurcher being particularly allergic to fleas. Tapeworm can also be a cause. Removal of the cause and an injection of antihistamine by the vet usually brings about an improvement.

Fleas

These should be dealt with immediately since, apart from being tiresome in themselves, they also serve as a host for tapeworm. They are best dealt with by means of an aerosol spray. The dog's sleeping area and bed must be thoroughly disinfested using as strong an insecticide as possible, usually an organophosphorus compound. *Do not* spray the dog with this preparation however but employ something milder.

Fractures

In lurchers the most commonly broken bones are the hock and the toes. Should a fracture be suspected, no time should be lost in contacting the vet meanwhile keeping the dog quiet and splinting the fracture using any stiff material which is to hand for this purpose such as wood, cardboard or leather.

Hard Pad

See distemper.

Inoculations

The puppy should be inoculated two weeks after it has been weaned against distemper, parvovirus and leptospirosis. The inoculant against all these diseases all of which are usually fatal, is contained in the single dose.

A booster should be given three to four weeks after the initial inoculation and annually thereafter.

Leptospirosis and Hepatitis
Kindred diseases of the liver frequently carried by rats. Inoculate as indicated above.

Lice
Blood sucking insects which lay their eggs (nits) on the dog's hair. They are controlled by insecticides in the same way as fleas, see above.

Mange
Follicular mange is difficult to cure and your vet should be consulted.

Sarcoptic mange is the more common variety. It is exceedingly contagious and can be readily transmitted to humans when it is known as scabies (five year itch). The best cure that I have discovered for both mange in dogs and human scabies is Benzyl Benzoate. This is fairly fierce sort of stuff and so should be applied to only one half of the dog's body in the first instance, the other half of its skin being treated three days later. Leave for a week and then wash off using warm soapy water. Repeat if necessary after an interval of three weeks. Benzyl Benzoate is also a very efficient controller of lice.

Mastitis
A complaint sometimes occurring in nursing bitches. Teats become swollen, hot and tender. Give a saline purge (Milk of Magnesia is good) and apply hot fomentations followed by local application of antibiotics for which the services of your vet will be required.

Muscles, Pulled or Torn
A common complaint in working lurchers. The only cure is complete rest and massage with embrocation. Green oils are an old fashioned shepherd's standby for many conditions and still constitute a remarkably efficaceous remedy. The best ones used to be manufactured by Thomas Pettifer and Son of Banbury but I think that this firm has been out of business for a good many years. Battles of Lincoln turn out a very good green oil nowadays.

Nephritis
Inflammation of the kidneys caused by a chill or by a stone in the kidney symptomised by a sudden attack of shivering and rise in temperature by as much as three of four degrees and a rapid pulse rate. Take no chances with this one and consult the vet as uraemic poisoning may ensue.

Parvovirus

A lethal and virulent disease usually attacking young puppies. It is highly infectious and must be inoculated against. See inoculations above.

Poisoning

The most frequent cause of poisoning these days is rat poison but some of the older mineral poisons still occasionally give trouble, the most common of these being the various salts of arsenic, lead and zinc. Gamekeepers in some parts of the country also continue to be not unacquainted with the use of strychnine. If your dog is known to have swallowed any of these substances, first aid should promptly be given in the form of an emetic to make the dog vomit. A tablespoonful of salt in half a cupful of water is perhaps the best known of the readily available emetics but a better one in my experience, is a piece of washing soda about twice the size of a hazel nut. Place this on the back of the dog's tongue and push it gently down its throat with your fingers. This should cause the dog to vomit. Then get the dog along to the vet without delay taking a sample of the poison along with you if this is possible.

Many poison substances occur in the countryside these days in the form of agricultural insecticides and herbicides. Take your dog to the vet without delay if you suspect it may have consumed any of these.

Rabies

Does not currently occur in the British Isles but is all too common in foreign countries and now we have the Channel Tunnel, who knows? It is a lethal disease of both man and beast and is conveyed usually by a bite but can also gain ingress to the body through any small cut or scratch. Incubation period is anything from three weeks to two years. The infected dog loses its appetite and becomes listless. Its voice will change to something between a bark and a howl; it will become morose and will bite everything in its path; furniture, bushes and other animals. Suspected cases should be closely confined (never shot) and the vet summoned with all haste.

Although anti-rabies inoculants have been developed these are by no means 100% reliable and the usual answer to an outbreak of rabies anywhere remains rigid control of domestic animals and mass destruction of wild species. The best prevention as far as we are concerned in this country is strict quarantine controls and anyone contravening these should be very heavily penalised indeed.

Snake Bite

Lurchers being naturally curious beasts are very apt to be bitten by adders where these exist, bites usually being suffered to the head and neck. All lurchermen should be able to recognise an adder. It is a flattish sort of snake with a black zigzag mark the length of the back. Should your dog be bitten get it along to the vet at once and he may be able to give it an injection of antivenom. As a first aid measure insert crystals of potassium permanganate into the wounds caused by the fangs. Keep the patient warm and quiet. Keeping up the body heat is particularly important in cases of snake bite.

Stings, Bee and Wasp

Remove the stings of bees by scraping out with a knife blade or the finger nail. Do not pinch the sting in any way as this will inject more venom into the dog. Swab with diluted ammonia.

Teeth

In the puppy there are 28 milk teeth. It drops these at the age of six months and acquires its permanent teeth, 42 in number. Give the dog marrow bones to chew in order to keep its teeth in good order. As the dog gets older, tartar may appear and this should be scraped off. Bad or loose teeth should be removed by the vet under an anaesthetic.

Ticks

Dogs will pick up ticks in some localities and these will be found usually during grooming when they may be removed. Forget about the possibility of leaving the creature's head behind and simply pull off the tick with your fingers. Once removed from the host it will not attach itself again and will simply crawl around until it dies. However, it is more satisfactory to destroy ticks and they may be flushed away or burned. In some of the wilder parts of the world in which I have lived this was usually brought about by the simple expedient of dropping the tick on to the hot top of a pressure lamp when it was lit, thus providing not only an efficient method of tick destruction but also a bonus of indoor fireworks in the shape of exploding ticks. I have not heard of ticks carrying any diseases of dogs in this country but have seen several cases of redwater caused by them in the tropics and so would be inclined to suspect them of being disease carriers in the U.K. as well.

Toe, Bruised

Keep the dog on its lead during exercise and immerse the foot in cold water at intervals during the day. If a great deal of pain is being caused the vet will cut back the nail in order to relieve pressure on it.

Travel Sickness

Dogs should be taken around in vehicles from an early age and they will thus become used to such travel. If however, your dog still suffers from travel sickness make sure that it is not fed before travelling. Tranquillisers have been tried but I have never heard of them doing much good.

Vomiting

This is a natural process in the dog in order to clear bile from the stomach and the dog will bring this about itself by eating various grasses.

Worms

Puppies should be regularly dosed for round worm as should the pregnant bitch. Follow the instructions on the bottle as different medicines may have different rates of dosage. Although they may sometimes have round worm, adult dogs are more prone to infestation by tapeworm. Lurchers should be dosed for tapeworm every 12 months and at any other time that segments appear in the faeces.

In order the better to deal with any of the emergencies which I have outlined it is a good idea to have by you a canine first aid kit. In addition to those medicaments which I have indicated it should also contain bandages, surgical needles and sutures, syringes, scissors and a thermometer.

Lastly I would just like to make a plea that when your dog is approaching the end of his days, whether due to old age, illness or serious injury, its life should be ended in as seemly and dignified a way as befits him or her. Try to be present when this happens and do not let him meet his end in the sole company of strangers at the end of a miserable and lonely sojourn, no matter how short, in some kennel which he has never seen before.

Problems

Like other dogs lurchers present us, their fond owners, with certain problems from time to time. I am going to describe a few of those which I have encountered, both in my own dogs and those of others, during the past 50 or so years, a period when there was seldom either a longdog or a lurcher far away.

OPENING UP

Of the difficulties which beset lurchers, and thus indirectly their owners, there are some which are peculiar to this type of dog. These are associated with the job a lurcher is required to do. Amongst these, probably the one which gives the most aggravation is the habit of opening up. For those who are not familiar with the term perhaps I had better explain that this is when a dog that is in pursuit of its quarry starts to give tongue. Not such a bad fault perhaps in these days when most of us are, or should be, law abiding and never to be found 'in pursuit of game' as the wording on the

The Pharoah Hound.

summons used to say when it was presented by our friendly neighbourhood copper to he whose dog had opened up, thus giving the game away
that hares were being exercised upon land where he had no right to be. It is
a tiresome habit nevertheless, even when the dog is being lawfully
employed, for the yelping of a dog can be relied upon to put all the game for
miles around below ground, should they be rabbits, and into the next field
but one if it is anything else.

So what are we to do about dogs which open up? This situation is one
where prevention is definitely better than a cure for only too frequently
cure there is none. Some breeds are particularly bad where this is
concerned, Ibizan and Pharoah Hounds having a reputation as being the
most notable performers in this respect. The reason for this is the way that
hunting is carried out in their native countries, where they are expected to

indicate their whereabouts in this manner, mute dogs being regarded with about the same amount of enthusiasm as might be a silent English Foxhound.

People come to me from time to time complaining that their hitherto faultless hunting companion has suddenly developed this irritating habit and I habitually address the same question to them, 'Has it been hunting alongside another dog?' The answer to this is just about always in the affirmative for this is the most frequent cause of opening up. Pack behaviour? communication? In my opinion it is simply frustration caused by the possibility of the other dog taking the quarry. Run two dogs together on the lamp and you may soon find out all about opening up. So the best method of prevention in this case is to run your dog on its own. But what about a cure?

The only cure is the obvious one of simply ceasing to run your dog at anything whilst there is another dog around, and hoping that this will do some good. In so doing, it would be as well if the other common cause of opening up were to be avoided. Again this is something which arises from frustration and occurs when a dog sees its quarry getting away from it. Always bear in mind that our canine chums, no matter how human they seem to be at times, are not capable of uttering the same expletives as are hissed sotto voce by their owners to give vent to all sorts of pent up emotions. Entering a dog to quarry before it is old enough to catch it can lead to opening up, as can trying to match a dog against a hare with which it is not capable of coming to terms. Fortunately the majority of sight hounds are silent hunters and they tend to pass this on to their offspring, but when the fault develops it is not often that it can be cured. One hears Grand Guignol tales about people having their dog's vocal chords removed by surgical means but one wonders where they managed to find a veterinary surgeon who would do the job, and so it is best to dismiss this piece of information as just another of the apocryphal tales with which lurchers seem to be surrounded.

WHINING

From one annoying and tiresome habit to another, which is of a similar nature, and that is whining. I am afraid that this is something that one simply has to become used to, should one aspire to becoming the owner of a lurcher or a longdog. Longdogs are, on the whole, worse for this than lurchers. So lurcher owners take what small crumbs of comfort that you can from this. It is as well if, irritated by this row, you do not put the dog outside into a kennel for then it is more than probable that its whine will develop into a full blooded howl leading to complaints from the neighbours and interference on the part of the Environmental Health Department. Luckily, although whining is another indication of frustration on the part of the dog, it is often the result of boredom through inaction and can rapidly be cured by taking it out and running it after something.

CHEWING

Chewing everything from your old slipper to the foot of the Queen Anne bureau is another source of annoyance. This is frequently encountered during puppyhood and usually disappears with the arrival of the dog's permanent teeth. If one is on the lookout for it, meanwhile keeping anything of value out of the dog's way during this period, it is a habit which most of them stop when they become adult, although there are some dogs which largely as a result of loneliness will persist in this sort of conduct all their lives. In its chronic form this problem is usually encountered in those households where the dog is left at home on its own for extended periods during the day when perhaps husband and wife are out at work and children at school. If someone can take the dog with them so much the better but should this not be possible, the best remedy is the acquisition of an indoor kennel. Despite their resemblance to a cage which tends to put some people off, dogs usually take to them very well and are content to lie there out of harm's way.

HARD MOUTH

Still dealing with the same portion of the dog's anatomy, its jaws, we come to the problem of hard mouth. Not a problem of much importance in guard dogs and terriers, it assumes considerably more importance in the context of the gundog and the lurcher, both of which are required to retrieve as part of their work. In the lurcher the matter of breeding comes into the picture and, as one might expect, terrier crosses tend to be harder in the mouth than do other sorts of lurcher. To say that this is always so would be a gross over generalisation, but the very nature of the various breeds of dog used in lurcher production is apt to highlight certain tendencies normally associated with whatever type of ancestry happens to be involved. However, I think that it would be only fair to say that more hard mouths develop in the course of a dog's working life than are the result of anything which might be handed down from its predecessors.

In my experience the easiest way of fostering a hard mouth in any lurcher is to hunt with it in company with other dogs, particularly terriers. Sooner or later kills will be disputed and hard mouths will not be long in making their appearance. In fact you will be lucky if this is the only result of such practices which if persisted in, will frequently lead to kills being thoroughly mutilated and perhaps, horror of horrors, eaten.

Overworking a dog as is only too easily done when working to a lamp, can also lead to the development of a hard mouth and to the man who

Overworking a dog as is only too easily done when working to a lamp, can also lead to the development of a hard mouth. This experienced lamper knows when to stop.

lamps in order to supply butchers or game dealers, this can be quite a serious problem. For the subsistence hunter hard mouths assume lesser importance. Most of the meat which is worth having on a rabbit carcase is on the back and the rear legs; the rib cage and front legs which are the most likely to suffer, are of little value. This is a fault you are unlikely to find a cure for, but having a dog which is sufficiently hard mouthed has at least one redeeming feature, this being that when it seizes its quarry the end is not prolonged. There is one very practical advantage of the rabbit's terminal squeals never being uttered. The horrid sound which otherwise ensues not only has the effect of broadcasting to all and sundry what is going on but will also have the effect of putting every other rabbit within earshot to ground.

As with so many other faults in an animal, things like this are easier to prevent than to cure. Even when prevention has failed if the problem can be spotted before it has had much of a chance to develop and the underlying cause identified, correction is possible in a great many cases. In my opinion a great number of the things which give us trouble with our lurchers are the results of too much company, both canine and human, when working. A lurcher always used to be the dog of the solitary hunter, the moucher, and as long as both owner and dog try to stick to this role, it will be found that a good deal less goes wrong.

THIEVING

One sometimes hears complaints of the thieving ways of lurchers. I am afraid that this is just one of those things at which any sighthound blooded dog always seems to excel and for which there seems to be no cure other than the somewhat draconian measures adopted by Parson Woodford, the eighteenth century Norfolk diarist who hanged his Greyhound for stealing a leg of mutton. Readers of *The Working Longdog* may remember the account of Shonks, the Wolfhound, whose favourite trick was to remove rice puddings from ovens whilst they were in the process of being cooked. No doubt there are others who could cap this tale for there are no thieving lengths to which a lurcher or longdog will not go. No cure as far as I am aware other than keeping edibles out of the dog's way.

WANDERING

Wandering is a habit which should be in no way encouraged. On the part of any dog it is tiresome enough but it is a serious failing in a lurcher which, as well as being more intelligent and with more tricks up its sleeve than other dogs, is also better able to surmount obstacles which might hinder lesser breeds. It can also be a footstep on the road to stock worrying. Your premises should of course be adequately fenced or the dog restrained in some other way but even then there are dogs which may wander off during the course of being exercised. Plenty of long walks taken at regular times of the day will usually prevent anything of this sort and such exercise is of course absolutely necessary from other aspects of management. Do not let the dog hunt out of sight and before thinking of taking it out other than on a lead make sure it has reached a stage in its training when it comes to you without any sign of hesitation whenever it is summoned. Although wandering dogs are nearly always indicative of something lacking in their management there are some which are particularly bad offenders in this way. Some bitches on heat, for instance, never let up on opportunities to escape signifying that they are ready and willing but the rest of the time are seldom tiresome in this way. Some dogs, as opposed to bitches, seem to be looking for a chance to roam at all times. As I have said, adequate exercise under supervision particularly at an early age is the overall answer but this is no substitute for dogproof fencing.

JUMPING UP

Many dogs when greeting their owners or their nearest and dearest and their acquaintances are apt to jump up on them. This can be particularly disconcerting in a lurcher which is long enough in the back to establish eye to eye contact. The shepherds and gamekeepers of my youth used to dissuade this sort of conduct by treading on the dog's rear feet, but apart from the cruelty involved, in a lurcher there is the distinct possibility of damaging its toes. The best way of discouraging this sort of behaviour is to have the dog on a lead whenever this situation might develop and when it jumps up, give the lead a very sharp tug, such as the dog is unlikely to forget. After it has experienced this once or twice it is not likely to try it on again.

CONCLUSION

These are a few of the problems which a lurcher owner will find himself having to face at times. There are plenty of others of course but with all faults the solution is often at hand simply by pondering the matter for a time and trying to think like the dog in order to arrive at the root cause of why the dog is doing whatever it is. From there it is often just a matter of working out a solution in many cases. Most bad habits if nipped in the bud will cause no more trouble but once let them develop and become reinforced in the dog's mind, they will usually take a great deal of dislodging. The old adage of prevention being better than a cure is just as true with dogs as with anything else.

— 8 —
Working

Entering to Quarry

RABBIT

The best, and usually the most readily available, quarry to enter a lurcher to is the rabbit. The majority of dogs, whatever their breed, are only too keen to chase rabbits. Indeed this is one of the rather more tiresome problems faced by the gundog trainer who has to train his charges not to run in to rabbit in much the same way as the rest of us train our dogs to leave farm livestock alone, even going to the lengths of having penned rabbits around so that their Spaniels and retrievers can become used to them. As far as lurchers are concerned all that you will need to do in most cases is simply to let the youngster see the rabbit. Its natural curiosity will then come to the fore and it will approach the unfamiliar object to take a closer look at it. The rabbit may be relied upon to depart with some degree of speed and canine nature being what it is, the pup will follow.

The first thing to ensure in entering your dog to rabbit will be that there are rabbits about. The best time of day for this is in the evening, or better still early morning when as well as rabbits being more likely to be abroad, less people may be expected to be around. You will probably know your ground fairly well but even if you do not, look for the odd rabbit which may have strayed that little bit further from home than the rest of its fellows.

At this stage of the proceedings your dog should be on the lead. In this way it will be you and not the dog who will select the target. As soon as you

Steven Robinson walking up rabbits with his Lurcher bitch, Holly, a Bedlington/ Whippet cross.

see a likely looking subject nicely away from cover and not too far away from you, slip the dog. Depending upon the time of year, of course, there is a possibility of finding a rabbit which is suffering from myxomatosis.

Should you see one then by all means let your dog have a go at it for by doing this you will be achieving two objectives; entering your pup and putting the unfortunate rabbit out of its misery. Don't worry about the disease; it is transmissible neither to dogs nor human beings.

Should you not come across a myxied animal it is quite likely that your dog will miss the first few rabbits at which it is run, but do not let this worry you too much. If it is one of the right sort it will not take long to start to work out angles of incidence and comparitive speeds and so on and will soon connect with its quarry. When it first does this it may well not know quite what to do with its catch and may try to hold it down with its feet. This is quite a natural thing at this stage and most dogs quickly learn the right way to pick up.

RAT

Should the dog persist in using its feet rather than its teeth there is one way in which this can usually be remedied fairly swiftly and this is to take it ratting. Dealing with quarry which is not slow to bite if not taken in the right way the dog generally learns what its teeth are for after a couple of encounters. In any case, it will be time by now for the dog to be entered to rat. A good ratting dog is well worth its keep and is a good means of introduction to farmers and gamekeepers. If you wish to pass yourself off as some sort of pest controller such a dog is an absolute necessity. The only drawback in the case of lurchers which do a fair bit of ratting is that this sometimes tends to cause them to be a bit hard mouthed. However, if you hunt for your own stew pot rather than for the sale of whatever you catch, a rabbit which is taken fairly positively is no great drawback. It is something which I am prepared to live with since any dog which I have must be capable of taking a fox where slight hardness of mouth is something of a plus attribute. The ideal, of course, is a lurcher who will use the correct amount of jaw power for each respective quarry, but as I have pointed out elsewhere in this book not all lurchers are perfect.

When first entering a lurcher to quarry it is necessary to play things by ear to a great extent. At most times it is better to work it on its own but there are other occasions when the presence of more experienced dogs can serve as both example and stimulus. Work it from the lead in the early stages. This will have the effect of leaving you in control of any situation that arises and will tend to make the dog all the keener to go.

LAMPING

As soon as it is picking up fairly regularly take it lamping. Some owners hold the opinion that the young entry is best started off on the lamp and this is one of those points over which lurchermen agree to differ to some extent. As with most other things it depends a good deal upon circumstances. If you intend to do a good deal of lamping entering it in this way would appear to be eminently sensible, but if this is not to be the case then it is more likely to acquire the right sort of habits by daylight entering.

HARE

Once your lurcher is taking rabbit satisfactorily you may experience an urge to enter it to hare. Now is a time for restraint for the hare is a very different type of quarry from the rabbit. Although superficially similar in appearance there is a deal of difference between the two species. One always assumes of course that you will not have it in your mind to try your dog at a leveret or a pregnant doe, neither of which can in any way be regarded as either sporting quarry or suitable meat for the pot. There are already plenty of the 'My dog caught a hare in July' sort about without adding to their pitiful throng.

A fully grown winter hare is fitting quarry for the best of dogs and as such should be left alone until your dog has attained his full growth at around two years. Unlike the rabbit with which a run of a hundred yards is quite a lengthy one, the hare is just nicely getting into gear at this sort of distance and will keep going for a very long time. How long you will find out if you ever follow beagles.

When coursing under rules, using Greyhounds in the peak of condition,

Many a hare is walked over, so effective is their use of camouflage and the lie of the land.

the hare will usually have the dogs' tongues hanging out before it goes through the hedge into the next field. Coursing Greyhounds usually leave off at this stage either because they have become unsighted or, as is nearly always the case, they are not very good at coping with obstacles such as hedges, fences and wide drainage ditches, all of which are of little concern to the lurcher, assuming that it has been properly trained. Such a dog is likely to carry on until it kills or else can go no further, having reached the point of exhaustion, a point which you yourself will have come to some time previously should you have been following the chase on foot. Not the sort of quarry to slip your young and comparatively inexperienced sapling on to for a hare will give a young dog a heart straining, lung bursting and muscle tearing run that could well leave it physically and mentally damaged for life.

Before entering to hare a lurcher should be two years old at least. By then, if you have so far done your job properly, it should be well muscled up and with bellows to match. Moreover, it will have had a year or so pursuing that elusive jinking target, the rabbit. It is not without reason that the owners of coursing Greyhounds try to keep their dogs away from rabbits for this is a fairly sure way of making them run cunning. A Greyhound that has learnt the skill of catching and killing hares is a certain loser on the coursing field where points are awarded for speed and turning the hare. It is one of the few field sports where the object is not to kill.

When you eventually enter your dog to hare take it along to a location where you expect there to be hares, and where you have the right to hunt them. Have it on a slip lead and walk the fields until a hare gets up. Strictly speaking, and under sporting rules, you should give the animal a hundred yards or so law before loosing your dog but in the circumstances of meeting your first hare, I feel that you might be forgiven for slipping a bit short. Once you have slipped, that should be the end of the matter for you, other than to ensure that your quarry, if caught, receives the dignity of a swift and unlingering end.

FOX

A lurcher entered to fox should, again, have attained its full growth. Some dogs are put off fox at their first encounter, even when they are big and strong enough to annihilate the creature. This makes them no less of a lurcher, although nothing of a foxing lurcher. Most dogs, however, particularly those with a good deal of longdog about them, and those which carry working terrier blood, are keen enough. One caveat though; it is just as well to be wary concerning a foxing lurcher's attitude to other dogs. A dog that is capable of killing a fox will have no problem in despatching a smaller dog if it has the inclination.

There are two different ways to enter a lurcher to fox. Firstly, at night using a lamp; secondly, by day, using a terrier to bolt a fox for the lurcher to course and kill.

FEATHER

An all round lurcher should be able to take feather as well as fur, but some are often reluctant to do so having been broken to chickens in no uncertain terms. The idea which you have to get into their heads is that there is a difference between these and certain other avian species. Many puppies if allowed, as they should be, to roam around the garden or other enclosed area will often make a dash at sparrows and pigeons. They will also do this when they are taken out for exercise. This should be encouraged. As part of your retrieving training, once the dog has mastered the business of bringing balls and similar objects to you, get it on to retrieving dead wood pigeons which you or your friends may have shot. At the same time curb any tendency to take too much interest in chickens or ducks. I know that this is easier said than done but it can be achieved, given sufficient patience and perseverance.

I have gone into the matter of entering at some length but their is a limit to what can be learned from a book. It is now time to have a go and be prepared to profit from mistakes, preferably those of others. As with training so with entering to quarry, which is merely an extension of that process, never allow yourself to be discouraged. Training is a lengthy and sometimes discouraging process, but if it is carried out thoroughly and conscientiously you will win in the end. A fully trained lurcher is a rare and precious thing and such will be yours. Once it is successfully entered to rabbit it can be regarded as made; the rest will usually follow in the fullness of time. Above all never be in too much of a hurry. To be too hasty is to court disaster.

Rabbiting, Lamping

Of all quarry taken by lurchers these days the rabbit must in numbers greatly exceed all else. In previous times, when there were considerably less lurchers about and most of their owners carried out their hunting on the land of other people, the usual quarry was the hare. Hunting in those days was for the pot and a hare would keep a working man's family in meat for a week. Rabbits were thought to be small fry to be run down by boys with sticks on the harvest field, and taken with ferrets and nets in the winter supplementing this with the use of the long net. Nothing, however, stands still and not only the ownership of lurchers but also their employment has greatly altered over the years since just after the end of the Second World War when myxomatosis appeared and chemical farming commenced.

The professional rabbit trapper of old regarded the use of any sort of dog for hunting down and catching a rabbit as something of a joke, a form of sport for the dilletante who could afford to do it that way. But nowadays I should think that it would be fair to say that more rabbits are taken on the lamp than by any other means. It is also a good deal more comfortable way of taking them than any of the old ways, which always seemed to entail an awful lot of kneeling down on wet grass and a good deal of work with a spade. The two easy options then were snaring and long netting, but even with these there was a good deal of humping equipment, not to speak of the catch, around.

Probably more rabbits are taken on the lamp by dogs than by any other means.

On the face of it there does not seem to be much to lamping rabbits, but any experience of it will soon show that some are a good deal better at it than others. Like most other things there are all kinds of little tricks and gimmicks that can spell out the difference between success and, if not failure, fairly partial success which is almost as galling.

PERMISSION

Assuming that you are starting off there are three things which you will require; a suitable dog, a satisfactory lamp and last but not least the land over which to hunt. Should you be one of the lucky few who own land the last item will take care of itself, otherwise you will have to obtain permission to hunt over someone else's. Whilst hunting rights are available in a good many places they are not always the easiest things to come by. Already knowing, or having an introduction, to some farmer who will let you on to his land is the best way, of course. Failing this, you will have to bring yourself to the notice of some one who is willing and able to do a deal of some sort.

What is the best way of going about this? Judging by the number of advertisements asking for rabbiting ground which appear in sporting periodicals, this is a fairly popular way of trying to break the ice but one wonders whether it is the best way. Far better to write to individual farmers; you can discover their names and addresses from the invaluable Yellow Pages. You could even telephone them but, should you do this, be careful to avoid mealtimes and those times when they might be watching their favourite TV programmes. Turning up unannounced at the farmhouse is not to be recommended. Farmers are pestered quite enough as it is by the purveyors of small seeds, crop sprays and so forth to welcome intrusions of this nature, and the majority of them will regard such a visit as an intrusion upon their privacy.

The best approach, to my mind, is still the good old standby, the local pub. Markets used to be admirable places for striking up acquaintanceships with likely sorts of persons but, due to stringent drink driving legislation and a general change in attitudes, country market town pubs are not the convivial centres of jovial intercourse which they used to be. Even in likely country pubs at the weekend you are more likely to discover that you are putting your sporting propositions to some green wellied yuppy than to anyone who can do any good for you. But this is still likely to be about the most fruitful venue.

Writing to individuals may stand a chance. If they want to see you, as they almost certainly will, should they be in any way interested, it is just as well not to appear in your favourite camouflage jacket with lurchers at heel. The soft approach often pays with no mention of dogs or night time hunting. Be prepared to start off with ferrets in hedgerows during the daylight hours. Once contact is made in this way, it is a good deal less troublesome to broach the matter of lamping at a later date.

You may, of course, be tempted to simply go ahead and lamp without permission relying upon the sharpness of your wits and the fleetness of your feet to keep you out of trouble. Whilst I am in no position to dictate to anyone what they should or should not do, I would simply say that I do not altogether advise such a course. I know that a large number of people purport to engage in this sort of illicit sporting activity, but unless there is direct and incontrovertible evidence of there having done so it is wise to weigh their words with caution. Potvaliant utterances are one thing, actually being seen to do the deed is another. Just remember that anyone flashing his lamp around fields in the middle of the night is broadcasting to all and sundry that he is there and what he is doing. I have done enough night work of various kinds to be well aware that he who makes no noise nor unnecessarily displays his whereabouts is the most likely to collect the goods, be it enemy prisoners or rabbits.

THE DOG

Now to the second factor in the general scheme of things, the dog. Again, it very much depends upon exactly what you want to do. Should you merely wish to catch a few rabbits for the pot, or for the pots of your suitably astonished friends and relations, it does not matter to any great extent what sort of dog you use. You may note that I keep on mentioning the animal as a dog and not specifically as a lurcher. This is because, in lamping, success depends to a great extent on the dog's intelligence in connection with working out such things as angles of impact and its stamina rather than on actual speed. Thus, just for taking the odd rabbit or two, nearly any sort of dog would do, and under this head I include such canine companions as collies and the larger terriers. However, you will probably be into this kind of hunting either from the point of view of pest control or as a supplement to whatever income you have. You may even be intending to make a living out of it. Not many people are able to do this but there are the few who can.

Let us assume that there are a large number of rabbits on your prospective hunting ground and that you are out to take as many as you possibly can. For this you will need a lurcher and, whilst it need not be remarkably fast, it should be able to get off at a fair speed but, above all, it must be possessed of a good deal of stamina. The sort of stamina which will enable it to make upwards of 30 runs in the course of a night's hunting. This implies some sort of lurcher which is big enough to stand the pace and I do not think that anything under about 21 inches would be much good for the job. There are exceptions of course but they just happen; they are not selected specifically for the job.

The animal should be good on the pick up and so you will not want too long a legged sort. This is where a Whippet scores over a Greyhound on straightforward rabbit catching; it takes its quarry from a totally different angle and hits it nearer to the horizontal rather than having to go down to

Lamping rabbits on a racecourse, one could hardly get a better running ground!

it. Anything over 23 inches is likely to be too tall for the job. This begins to narrow the options a bit.

Nose? Well, opinions do tend to vary a bit on this score but my own is that the less sense of smell a lamping dog has, the better at the job it will be. The last thing that you want to happen is for the dog to miss its target on the initial run and then start to hunt it by scent. This can be a very great nuisance in the dark, since your lurcher following up some rabbit by the use of its nose with a destination of no one knows where, will soon put a whole field of rabbits to ground.

Your ideal lamping dog should have a good weatherproof coat for the very nature of what you are doing will take you out on nights when weather conditions are frequently at their most foul and the last thing that anyone wants at such times is a dog by their side which is shivering with cold. Neither can the dog give of its best in such circumstances. To this end you will not want an animal with a fine smooth coat nor will you want one which has a soft woolly sort of texture to its coat for this will hold the moisture in such a way as to make the dog even more cold than if it had a smooth coat. The thing to aim for is the dog with a strong broken coat, the kind that will easily shoot off the water as soon as the lurcher shakes itself. Equally useful is the thick smooth coat which some lurchers have. This is just about as good as the broken coat.

I have listed the points for which I would be on the look out were I trying to find my ideal lamping dog. What sort of breeding would provide me with the paragon for which I would be looking? In my own case, it would come down to a Greyhound crossed either once or twice but not more than twice, with a good working sort of Bedlington or collie.

There are those who use everything from a Saluki down to the diminutive Bedlington/Whippet for lamping and swear by them. A good deal of it would seem to depend upon just how serious a lamper you are likely to be.

THE LAMP

Having considered the dog for such work, let us pause for a minute to consider the remaining part of the gear, the lamp itself. Every year, nay just about every month, sees a new sort of lamp coming on to the market so that, by now, these come in all shapes and sizes. To purchase the most expensive does not necessarily mean that you are purchasing the best for the job. There are quite a number of lamps to be had which have very evocative names which I shall not quote. All sorts of extravagant claims are made on behalf of some of them, but look before you leap and then, having thought a bit about the matter, look again.

What does it matter whether the Patent Purple Death Ray can project a beam to illuminate objects at a mile and half's distance. All manner of obstacles can get in the way, not excluding the curvature of the earth. Also you would not wish to run your dog at something much over a couple of hundred yards away for very obvious reasons, number one being that its performance might be expected to be falling off a bit by the time that it reached its target.

Another consideration where the ultra long range type of lamp is concerned is that of the state of the weather. On the whole, the best sort of night for lamping is a windy, murky maybe wet sort of one when the elements may be relied upon to nullify the effects of the strongest beam of light. It is also an incontrovertible fact that a long-range beam is necessarily a narrow one. Not the best of illumination in which to run a rabbit, for as well as the difficulties of keeping the rabbit within the beam of the lamp I find such high powered pieces of equipment a trifle confusing to the dog. Well, my dogs anyway; it may be different where these superdogs are concerned, about which one reads in letters to the sporting press from time to time.

The most useful lamp that I have found and, although I do not do much rabbiting on the beam, I take a fair amount of foxes with it, is the sort of thing which is usually sold as part of what is described as a Complete Lamping Outfit with a 55 watt quartz halogen lamp of 250,000 candlepower which is driven by a 6.5 amp hour battery. Given the option I would opt for a Gel Battery which is non-spill, since generally speaking this will give less trouble than a lead acid battery. Such a lamp, whilst not providing an unnecessarily wide beam will give one which will provide you with a good deal better idea of what is going on than one of the high intensity jobs.

A good deal has been heard about red filters – not to be confused with infrared lamps – in recent years. The general notion seems to be that you are able to shine a red filtered lamp around without disturbing whatever quarry that you happen to be after. Well, that be as it may; I have never found such things to be of much assistance, myself. I have tried one out not only on rabbits but also on fox and on rats in a building. The effect on the quarry in each instance was so minimal as to be unnoticeable but the effect on me was such that I found it difficult to distinguish any objects at all in something closely resembling a cosy fireside glow. The filter makes quite a handy shield, however, for saving the glass of the lamp itself from getting too badly scratched and so it must be worth having from that point of view.

THE WEATHER

Well, we have touched upon the ground, the dog and the lamp and so let's have a look at the weather, that supposedly never ending topic of conversation between members of the great British Public. In a nutshell, be it never so vile it can scarcely ever be vile enough for the requirements of the lamper to rabbits or fox. A howling gale with a touch of cutting hail and sleet on the teeth of the wind is just about right. Of course, like all good things this is something which upon occasion can be taken a bit too far. At a latish hour on the night of 15th October, 1987 a young acquaintance of mine decided that, since the wind was getting up, this would be an excellent time to go out with his lamp and his lurcher in pursuit of rabbits in a secluded valley at the top of the North Downs. He arrived at his hunting ground a little after midnight and, even in the sheltered location where he was, he thought that the wind was somewhat stronger than usual, but it was not until he decided that things were getting a good bit rougher than he had anticipated at about 2 a.m. on the morning of the 16th and made a move for home that he discovered just how inclement the weather had become. This was the night or rather early morning of the hurricane which hit south east England.

His valley, the whereabouts of which he always keeps secret, must occupy a particularly cosy part of the landscape for it was not until he arrived back at his van with trees crashing down all about him, and twigs and other bits of timber flying around like bullets, that he realised the full extent of the situation. Knowing the countryside around there like the palm of his hand, having hunted over it since his schooldays, he was able to extricate himself from the place and eventually to get back home without injury to himself, his dog or his vehicle which was something of a feat in itself. Personally, I think that this is pushing things a bit and, as far as I am concerned, Force 8 is about optimum.

The blacker the night the better and for this reason, a night of low cloud with or without its usual accompaniment of squally rain is to be preferred. If there is plenty of cloud it does not much matter about the state of the moon. Moonlight or not, there is so much glare from the sky reflection of street lighting all over most parts of Britain that dense cloud cover is about the only state of affairs to ensure a really dark night. For the lamper there is no delight whatsoever in the shiny night.

However, this is not to decry the shiny night as seems to be the fashion amongst some self styled country pundits these days for, with all due respect to them, they do not even know what it is that they are decrying. I will freely admit that for lamping or for long netting a dark night is a necessity but for flighting wild duck a moonlight night somewhere near to the full with the accompaniment of plenty of low but not too dense cloud cover creates nearly perfect conditions. Perfect conditions also for spotting roosting pheasants, or so I am reliably informed. But, as I have said, for lamping rabbits the dark and stormy night is best.

TIME

Well, we now have the dog, the lamp and the night and so let us not hang around any longer for it is time to get up and go. What time? you may justifiably enquire, to which the answer must be that you should forget about it in the early part of the evening, and particularly in that part of it which happens to be the hour after the pubs chuck out. This is the hour of the pot valiant poacher, the bar room boaster, whose colossal bags of game are frequently not much more than products of his own overheated imagination. Wait until one o'clock, better still two o'clock in the morning for by this time things will have quietened down a bit, lulling your quarry into the nearest thing to a state of false security that it is ever liable to attain.

There will not be many people about either at this time, just the odd car going along the road as someone proceeds homewards after having given his girlfriend one more hug. Quite apart from the main consideration of your prey being more readily taken by now, it is a great time to be abroad with the feeling that the world belongs to you for a few small hours. Make the best of it for it is a condition which cannot last for long. Walk to your chosen hunting ground, should this be within reasonable distance, for motor vehicles are the enemies of peace and quiet which should be forming the basis of all your activities at this particular time. If you have to go wherever you are going by car or van, then leave it well away from what is to be the scene of your activities, ensuring that it is off the road and is in as unobtrusive a position as possible, for malicious individuals have been known to let down the tyres and tamper with the mechanics of vehicles which they happen to discover lying about in the middle of the night, even going to the extent of purloining all the wheels.

SLIP LEAD

Let us assume that you have progressed so far and are at the scene of operations. One dog should be quite enough and this should be on a slip lead or quick release collar of some kind. Not, I would advise, the makeshift slip of a length of baler twine looped through the dog's collar which is favoured by some. Running dogs work better when they are unimpeded by collars and there is always the possibility of a dog getting hung up on some snag and choking itself. Quite apart from the welfare of the dog, there is also that of yourself to be considered.

Even quite a short period with the baler twine cutting into your hand will rapidly incline you to the opinion that those who advocate such methods have not perhaps spent very long out doors at night with straining lurcher on one hand and lamp on the other in search of conies.

You may, of course, be one of those who has a dog so well trained that it runs from the 'At Heel' position and, therefore, does not require a collar or lead. If this is so, count yourself as both brilliant and fortunate for you are one in a thousand. Most lurchers of any worth, however, have to be restrained in the presence of game. If you have experience in the field of competitive coursing under rules you may have encountered hounds which hang back in the slips and you will be only too well aware how they run, or rather do not run.

WALKING THE FIELD

Having completed the preliminaries, probably the best way to walk up a field is about 30 yards out from the hedgerow with the wind in your face. If there is a wood or plantation on this side of the enclosure, so much the better. Forget all misconceptions regarding a rabbit remaining frozen in the beam; it may possibly crouch down, but it is more likely to high tail it

'Forget all misconceptions regarding a rabbit remaining frozen in the beam'. A rabbit attempts to get away at full speed with the Lurcher close behind.

for its burrow once the light is on it. The only advantage that you have is not that you can dazzle your quarry but that you can catch it further away from home than would be the case during the hours of daylight. So switch on your lamp and see what there is about. Should there be a rabbit well out from the hedge and not too far away, slip your dog on to it. If nothing is to be seen, quickly switch off and walk on a bit, then try again. Just as long as your dog has been properly trained it should get hold of the idea swiftly enough, connect with its quarry and retrieve it to hand.

It may well miss, more probably sooner than later, in which case try not to be dispirited but have another go. This is the time when you may be glad that your ideal lamping dog has very little nose for, if it had, it would probably start to hunt up, putting down everything in the field. A dog with little sense of smell will usually give up on missing its target and return to heel.

ENTERING TO LAMP

Opinions differ as to whether it is better to enter a dog directly to work on the lamp or whether to give it a certain amount of experience of hunting in daylight first. I incline to the latter view myself for once a young dog has realised that when he misses his rabbit it goes to ground, he will be less inclined to hang around looking for it when he misses. At the same time I believe that, should the lurcher owner be doing a good deal of lamping, it is just as well to restrict his dog to this sort of work. It will then improve fairly rapidly and, if it is the right sort of dog, it will eventually connect with just about every rabbit at which it is slipped. In the case of anyone who indulges in a spot of lamping from time to time, but who is in no way serious about it, then I would recommend starting it in daylight and aim to become the owner of an all round dog.

When out lamping be prepared for rather more than the average amount of wear and tear on the dog, for in the dark it will not have anything like the same degree of all round vision that it has in the daytime. This means that it is more likely to run into obstacles like trees, posts and fences causing all manner of injury, from bruises to a broken neck but mainly cuts from barbed wire. It is imperative that your dog should be a competent jumper and that it should have had experience of going over the current fashion in rural fencing, pig netting with a strand of barbed on top. This is where a thorough schooling in clearing obstacles with all four feet rather than crawling over the top of them will score, for then the dog is more liable from experience to realise the nature of a wire fence.

These then are a few thoughts on the subject of lamping but, like most things, this is something best learned by experience. By all means go out with someone else for a start to see how it is done but, should no one be keen to take you, do not allow this to deter you from having a go on your own. In any case, get into the habit of working on your own as soon as you can for, like most other things connected with hunting, to go out mobhanded is a fairly sure formula for failure. The exceptions to this are fox or hare hunting with packs of hounds or beagles, although even then three or four persons; Master, huntsman and two whippers-in will be quite sufficient in reality.

Should your efforts with the lamp be crowned with success, as well they might be, for it is a game at which the beginner occasionally excels the veteran, do not be tempted to return to the same place the following night to endeavour to emulate your performance. You might just well do so if you are hunting upon fresh ground but sooner rather than later you will discover that as soon as you enter the field, let alone switch on your light, every rabbit within both earshot and eyeshot will be straightway into cover. Hunt the same ground as infrequently as you possibly can for rabbits, like all quarry species, very rapidly learn to associate human manifestations with danger. It is difficult to say whether it may be possible to hunt the same ground as frequently as once a week but this rough yardstick should be regarded as an absolute maximum.

In the same way, do not let success go to your head in such a fashion as to lead you to overtax your dog. More than one lamper has discovered that he has the perfect dog for the job and the perfect conditions for running it, but just as he is congratulating himself on his enormous bag for the night, his pride and joy collapses and expires before his very eyes. To let this happen is not only the mark of the crass amateur but also the sign of the man who has no feeling for his lurcher whatsoever. Such a person would be better employed sitting by his fireside watching the exploits of others on the television.

Rabbiting, Daylight

If you are a ferreting man, or have inclinations in this direction, a well trained lurcher can be of considerable assistance. The sort of dog which is best suited to this kind of work is the smaller sort, probably one with a fair amount of Whippet blood. You are not after the stamina and staying power of the lamping lurcher but rather the lightning initial acceleration of a dog that is into top gear within the first couple of yards. A terrier/Whippet cross is just about ideal, something which is not over about 22 inches. Three-quarter Whippet and a quarter Bedlington would do very nicely, although I have seen plenty of the tiny first crosses of this blood which are absolutely lethal on rabbit. There are considerably more of these crosses advertised nowadays than there were a few years ago.

FERRETING

There are some ferreters who rely entirely on their dogs to catch the bolted rabbits, but there is very little doubt that by doing it this way a good many rabbits are lost. However, as a sporting pursuit, it takes a good deal of beating. This means one can operate on a one dog and one ferret basis, thus doing away with the necessity of carting a lot of heavy bits and pieces around, but I would reiterate that this is where you are doing your rabbiting more as a matter of providing yourself with entertainment than anything else. The right sort of ferret will travel in your pocket or a light ferret bag, and with dog at heel away you go. However, should you be hunting rabbits for the reason that you are pestered by them or because you are trying to make a living at it, then you will have to be prepared to sally forth with a good bit more in the way of equipment.

The professional rabbit catcher has always relied upon two 'engines' which is how they are described in various of the Game Laws. These consist of the snare and the net. Snaring is a comparatively effortless method of catching rabbits but, despite the fairly large catches which can be accomplished, it is to a certain extent limited which is where ferreting comes into the picture. Very few of the old professional warreners and

The regular rabbiting man, will use his dog as an adjunct to his purse nets.

rabbit catchers had much use for dogs; they relied upon their ferrets and carefully set nets to achieve the spectacular results of those days. Any rabbit catcher who, cap in hand, approached the head keeper on any of the large estates of those days, would have been certain of receiving short shrift were he to arrive looking for favours with any sort of dog at heel. Should it have been a lurcher or even a Whippet or a Bedlington Terrier he would have received even less in the way of an enthusiastic welcome.

Today's rabbit catcher is rather a different kettle of fish but it should still be remembered that old prejudices linger and that although the days of the large heavily keepered estate has, to a very large extent, disappeared no shooting man fancies having a dog disturbing his nesting pheasants. It is therefore paramount that the ferreter's dog should be trained to absolute perfection. The professional, or at any rate the regular rabbiting man, will use his dog as an adjunct to his purse nets as well as a useful indicator as to whether a particular burrow is occupied. This state of affairs is not such a difficult one to attain as it might sound.

Personally, were I to be going around in the hopes of finding a bit of rabbiting land on a vermin control sort of basis, I would not have a lurcher which went beyond the first cross and the more that it resembled a collie or some sort of mongrelly terrier, the better, just as long as it had a moderate turn of speed.

To my mind the most useful function of such a dog is to indicate whether a burrow is occupied. Most dogs are capable of doing this and do not take much in the way of training to do it, once they have been taken out ferreting a time or two. The main thing to guard against is over enthusiasm, manifested in its most extreme form by the dog digging its way into the burrow and trying to usurp the function of the ferret. A dog which snuffles and whines around the hole is also one which will very quickly prove to be more bother than it is worth. The dog should merely mark to earth, nothing more.

This is always assuming that your rabbiting lurcher has already been conditioned to ferrets, for the worst thing that could possibly happen would be for the ferret to pop its head out of one of the rabbit holes only to be nailed by your dog. This seems to be such an elementary point that it is scarcely worth mentioning but, nevertheless, it is something that sometimes occurs. It is an easy enough situation to avoid simply by letting your lurcher pup get together with a ferret. Let them out together and, as a rule, they will get along with one another from the outset although just occasionally a pup, particularly if it happens to have any terrier blood, may decide to give the ferret a nip. This is the time that it swifly learns that this is not all that good an idea. In the days when I did a fair bit of ferreting to rabbits I conditioned all my pups, both lurchers and terriers, by putting them on the ground with a good old hob ferret. He was a master at making good lads or lasses as the case might happen to have been and in

The model ferreting dog, a Bedlington/Whippet cross, sits calmy watching the other entrances to the warren.

no time at all both ferrets and pups would be feeding from the same dish. This is not a difficult state of affairs to achieve and, should you be intending to use any sort of dog to assist you in your ferreting endeavours, this is something about which you must be sure beyond any doubt before you even consider making a start. Once they have been properly introduced to one another, lurchers and ferrets usually get on well enough for both are intelligent creatures and will fairly soon come to realise that each is there in order to complement and assist the other.

As well as marking to occupied burrows, the lurcher should be able to make a further contribution by being able to pick up such rabbits as will inevitably find the one bolt hole which has not been netted, or slip around a net which has been set anything less than perfectly. Your dog should be trained to sit or lie down quietly whilst waiting for a rabbit to bolt. Wandering about and following its own devices to the detriment of giving its full attention to what is going on is in no way acceptable in the ferreting man's dog.

BUSHING

Another way in which rabbits may be caught during the hours of daylight is by driving them out of patches of brambles and briars, a practice commonly referred to as bushing. Many more rabbits lie out in such cover than did so in the days before myxomatosis began to take its toll. This, I am sure, increases their chances of survival as those which lie out in this way rather than going to ground are less likely to come into contact with the myxomatosis carrying rabbit flea which infests the burrows.

Bushing can provide excellent sport although it is unlikely that a very large bag will result from catching rabbits in this way. For the subsistence hunter, the man who requires a couple of rabbits now and then for his own consumption it represents a fairly trouble free way of accomplishing this object. Mention bushing to many lurchermen and they will immediately start thinking in terms of lurcher and terrier combinations, the usual procedure being to loose a few terriers into a bramble patch while stationing one or two lurchers around the perimeter of the cover so as to be able to pick up anything which emerges. Whilst being all very well in its way, this method of doing things is not without its drawbacks, the main one being the jealous disposition of just about every worthwhile terrier. This frame of mind will almost certainly, sooner or later, lead to disputed catches, which in turn may result in fighting with perhaps a dead terrier as the result. Another problem that can arise is that the lurcher is very likely to be put right off retrieving, to be followed by the lurcher starting to consume its quarry. This is a grievous fault which can also arise from simply running two dogs together, just as can opening up.

The most effective way of bushing with a lurcher is to take your dog on its own to the scene of your projected activities. Before doing do, however, make sure that you are yourself equipped with something substantial in the way of footwear and trousers, something with a bit more timber in them than trainers and blue jeans. Heavy hobnailed working boots are just about ideal as are nether garments of stout Derby tweed, the sort that you stand up in the corner rather than hang over a chair at the end of the day. Wellies are out unless they are an old pair which are past praying for and which it will not matter if you puncture, for in thorns this is exactly the thing which you are most apt to do to them. The old leather leggings, or buskins as they were called in some places, were the things for this job but, a common piece of country clothing 50 years ago, I do not know where anyone might go for a pair these days.

Having rigged yourself out in this fashion you will be ready to take over the role of the terrier, not of course by creeping terrierlike under the cover but by attacking it from above. Your dog, if it has been properly trained, should readily mark to rabbits in cover and then it is up to you to wade into the middle of the thorns and poke around with the long ashplant, which should also be an indispensable part of the working lurcherman's gear. When I say poke around with your stick this is exactly what I mean; it is no good threshing about in cover in the vain hopes of bolting rabbits many of which will simply sit it out and be beaten to death when one small poke with the end of a stick will be enough to dislodge all but the most stubborn.

A three-quarter Whippet/Collie owned by John Bayles, an excellent bushing dog.

Whilst engaged in any form of hunting, be it by day or by night, never forget the wind; it can be either your enemy or your ally. Not only does it carry the scent of both yourself and your dog but it also carries every little sound to the ears of your quarry the hearing of which is super acute in most cases. Although the eyesight of those animals which we hunt is far from faulty it never seems to reach quite the same pitch of perfection as the other senses.

Thus, when your dog marks to cover, station it in such a way that the wind if any, blows from the undergrowth towards the lurcher. Then quietly go round to the other side of the bushes and when opposite your dog you may make as much of a noise as you like. This should have the effect of moving the quarry in your dog's direction. At all other times go as noiselessly as you are able, this being yet another good reason for hunting on your own. *Always be positively aware of the wind direction.* As long as you have it in your face you will not go far wrong either by day or when you are lamping at night.

There are some lurchers, particularly the Whippet based ones, which are just as at home in cover as are a good many terriers. Being able to hunt

139

out undergrowth and hedge bottoms is a very useful quality in a lurcher, just so long as it is the sort that does not become too immersed in the hunting to the neglect of all else and keeps its wits about it ready for anything to bolt. The only snag is that such dogs are sometimes a bit apt to get hung up in the cover and so do not get quite such a good run at their quarry. I think that on balance this is something with which I would be prepared to put up with to a certain extent, assuming that the lurcher connects with its rabbit in the majority of instances.

Some of these dogs become adept at killing in and then retrieving from cover. One Bedlington/Whippet which I knew was first rate at this, and also took moorhens, coots and got into the habit of fetching fish out of streams, thus proving himself as a complete all round provider. I have yet to meet another lurcher with this piscatorial capability, although I dare say that it is something that might be taught to a dog of Labrador type.

Hares

Hares can be a confounded menace to farmers particularly when present in large numbers. It used to be reckoned that three hares ate just about as much as one sheep and, in root crops, damaged considerably more than they consumed. Hares are strange creatures and our Saxon ancestors believed that such beings as Were-hares existed. They tend to be very territorial animals. I recollect hares being almost everywhere in my youth, and while this may simply have been due to my boyhood having been spent in Lincolnshire and my immediate post-school years in Norfolk it is certainly the case today that they can be present in considerable numbers in one particular locality whilst a few miles away on similar land, farmed by the same man, they are non-existent.

Both beagling and coursing, whilst providing sport and healthy exercise for their followers have never been much use in the control of hare populations. The usual solution to the problem of too many hares has been a hare drive to guns. When such events take place and large numbers are destroyed it does not seem to lead to any appreciable diminishing of numbers in the following year. The few that are taken by lurchers can, therefore, have but a minimal effect on long-term population levels. I am convinced that the Game Conservancy have got it right when they put small hare counts in any locality down to there being large numbers of foxes present and a loss of habitat. The estate upon which I was brought up had, for some reason unknown to me, no fox hunting over it. Such foxes as appeared, from time to time, were ruthlessly hunted down by gamekeepers and shot, for the pheasant was paramount. We always had huge quantities of hare, which indeed posed a nuisance of no small dimensions, particularly amongst fodder root crops during winter.

There occurs from time to time a certain amount of controversy as to whether or not a lurcher or longdog can take hares single handed. This is habitually conducted on the lines of, 'No, you didn't'; 'Yes, I did,' a level of debate most of us left behind with our primary schooldays. Of course, it all depends upon what you mean by a hare; it also depends upon what you mean by a lurcher and also what you mean by that little matter which most of us refer to as 'law'. Not the law of the country or even that of the jungle but of how much start you are prepared to give to the hare. In coursing under rules this is normally an estimated one hundred yards, but when hunting for the pot or, in the bad old days, as an antidote to starvation, it was considerably truncated, often to the point of a dog picking up a hare from its seat.

Most of the dogs used in so called 'best of three' contests are not lurchers

John Bayles with his Lurcher, Tip, who is an excellent size and shape for coursing hares, which he does admirably.

but longdogs. A few years back, the Deerhound/Greyhound cross was very popular for this sort of activity but recently it has become an almost sine qua non that a 'best of three' dog must have a very large helping of Saluki blood. This must be due in part to the increasing popularity of Salukis but I feel it is also a reflection of how demand has grown for a specialist dog which will excel at one specific event. In fact, the use of lurchers generally is becoming compartmentalised and there seems to be one sort for lamping, another for ferreting, another for foxing and yet another for hare coursing. The so-called all round lurcher could easily become a thing of the past. As something of a traditionalist I think that this is a pity.

It is as well to remember that the word 'hare' covers not only the exceedingly athletic winter hare in full possession of all its many faculties but also anything from small leverets to pregnant does, as well as a few old hares getting past their prime. I seem to hear more people talking about how many hares their dog has taken over the weekend during the summer than at any other time of the year, and it does not require much of a stretch of the imagination to figure out why. There is no credit to be had from taking leverets and pregnant does. If your dog takes a winter hare that has been given proper law then you have something to boast about.

The going can also considerably influence the outcome. Given some nice compact turf particularly if the enclosure contains a few natural obstacles, the dice can be loaded very much in the hare's favour whereas matters assume a very different complexion in a young cereal crop which is getting a fair amount of growth on. The different combinations of circumstances are, of course, innumerable which all makes a bit of a nonsense of such statements as, 'My dog caught x number of hares on Sunday morning.' It is, incidentally, illegal to course hares on a Sunday.

How does one catch the sort of hare that was reputed to feed an agricultural labourer's family for a week? A good many such hares were taken in snares set in hedgerows and set too high for rabbits, others were taken in gin traps which had been set quite unlawfully in the open. Gin traps themselves are now classed as illegal engines and snaring in hedgerows becomes considerably more difficult with the disappearance of quickset hedges. There remains the lurcher and the meat hunter will not be too scrupulous about giving the hare any law whatsoever, the dog picking it up in its seat when this is possible. Any dog which is sufficiently powerful to hold a hare will be capable of doing this. In fact, many a shepherd's collie has proved itself very good at the job. It is much more a matter of guile than of speed.

To a person badly needing a square meal, a hare is not a terribly difficult animal to catch. This is the reason that any form of organised sport which consists of pursuing them is hedged about with rules, all of which are specifically designed for the hare's survival so that the creature will be there to run another day. Nevertheless, an appreciable few of them are still taken by beagles, the hunting of which is ordered at a very steady pace. Just remember this the next time that the chap next to you in the beer tent at the lurcher show is boasting about the number of hares which he took last week with his high powered lurcher.

Hares may, of course, be taken on the lamp in much the same way as rabbits. In fact they are easier than rabbits to take on the lamp. Unlike a rabbit which merely has his whereabouts illuminated by it the hare seems to be entirely put off its stroke by the lamp and will simply go loping away at a steady pace in front of the beam, presenting a sitting target for even the least accomplished running dog. I have even known occasions when the hare has run back into the lamp showing signs of genuine confusion. There is too much of the sitting duck about the thing to seriously merit the attention of anyone who has any pretensions to sportsmanship and, in this overall description, I even include those with empty bellies. There must be some better way of filling them in this day and age.

Fox

Of all the quarry to which a lurcher may be put I regard the fox as being one of the most worthwhile. With a few notable exceptions those foxhunts which operate in this country manage between them to account for remarkably few foxes. It has always seemed to me that the tally of foxes killed depends to a very great extent upon whether anyone wants to control the number of foxes or whether they just want to look cute when riding to hounds. There would therefore appear to be more scope for the fox-hunting lurcherman in one of the counties where they ride to hounds

A fox at full stretch for the nearest cover.

than there would be for instance in Cumbria with its very efficient foot packs.

To be perfectly fair about the matter, foxhound packs do have a good deal to endure. Railways have been with them for more than a century but it is only during the last 50 years that most of these have been electrified making them a hazard to hounds for one hundred per cent of the time, instead of merely when the train was coming. Added to this more and more motorways with more and more feeder roads have been built, and new housing developments continue apace for those whose main mission in life seems to be to fill up the roads and railways. Everyone rushes everywhere at ever increasing speeds, each in his lemming like way, and country pursuits of every kind can only suffer. Of these by far the greatest casualty must be fox hunting. I think that the next few years will see the demise of more than one old established pack in the South of England. To a certain extent the fox hunting lurcher owner is beset by the same problems, but the difference in the methods of hound handling will allow him to continue where the foxhound pack is defeated by the progress of civilisation, or what passes for it.

One is fully aware that hunting with lurchers is not without its hazards and seldom a year goes by without one hearing about some running dog being mown down by traffic whilst in pursuit of quarry of some kind or other, but, on the whole, the lurcher operator is better able to choose his ground than is the hunter to hounds. He is also in a better position to halt his dog if he sees it running into danger, although any sort of canine takes a bit of stopping when it is on a hot scent, or even more so when running in view. Also the laws of probability being what they are, one dog belting across a busy road stands a proportionately better chance of escaping unharmed than does a pack of perhaps 26 couple.

The lurcher owning fox hunter will, by the very nature of his craft, also be very much less likely than the organised foxhunt to suffer from the unwelcome attentions of hunt saboteurs and their kin. All this allows him to get on with the job and may be part of the reason why the efforts of lurchermen and terrier operators are so conspicuously more successful than those of their scarlet coated brethren.

Foxes are taken by lurchers mainly in two different ways; lamping during the hours of darkness and bolting them, or digging them out, with the aid of terriers. The lie of the land has a fair bit to do with whichever method is preferred, night hunting with a lamp being favoured in the more intensively farmed localities, whilst bolting the fox is the better way of doing the job in more open situations.

To be fairly sporting about it all, neither of these methods of vermin control should be carried out during the breeding season between the months of March and November, which is just as well, should you intend to lamp for fox, for this is the time of the year when the corn is beginning to grow and the foxes are beginning to lie out in it. However, should you happen to be the owner of sheep or poultry in a locality which is over foxed you will be unlikely to take quite such a sporting and open minded attitude towards the matter. Most of us have heard by now, and goodness knows it has been sufficiently publicised, the view of the antis and the loony left on the subject of predation by foxes. For those who have not, why should they not be permitted to have some sort of sardonic chuckle about it like the rest of us. According to these people foxes only consume dead cadavers in their role of universal scavengers. Confronted with the fact that the fox has been seen in the act of stalking a freshly dropped lamb, or in the act of emerging from the fowl run with one of your best laying hens carried at the high port, the answer of the conservation at all costs merchants just has to be, 'Well, it must have been some sickly specimen which would have died anyway.' This is the clever as opposed to informed reply.

Those of us who have had any experience of livestock breeding and rearing are bound to have a very different view and will continue to control foxes to a reasonable sized population unlike the antis, who would like to see none at all killed, and quite a lot of the foxhunting fraternity, who seem to regard the matter similarly although for a different reason. Really, at the base of it all, it is quite astonishing how the two, apparently opposed, camps of fox hunters and anti blood sports people can be so antagonistic for they are both engaged in a similar activity, the preservation of foxes at all costs.

There cannot be much doubt by now that owing to this kind of outlook the fox population has proliferated to the point where the creatures are a menace to many forms of livestock.

The only course open to the rest of us, who seem at least to be preserving some sense of reality in the matter, is to maintain the fox population at a sensible level. Should the fox hunters arguments triumph we could swiftly be overrun with the things whilst, should the antis have their way, and the fox be made a protected species, as with the badger it will automatically be gassed in its earth by the men from the ministry on some pretext.

BOLTING

So, let us consider the alternatives that we have at our disposal for the better control of foxes. By far the best way, given the right sort of country, is to nip the problem in the bud and to destroy them in or near their earths. This is one of the times that you will have to rely to a very large extent, in fact probably entirely, upon the services of a good terrier for the working terrier is to the fox hunting man what the ferret is to the rabbiter.

The drill, basically, goes something like this. Lurcher, if it is the right fox hunting sort marks a fox to earth or, alternatively, the terrier does so. Terrier is put into hole. Fox bolts and is taken by lurcher. However, life is not simple and the life of the pest controller is even less simple than most.

In the first place, the question arises, 'When is a fox earth a fox earth?', and the answer to this is not altogether straightforward, for the creatures are apt to occupy just about any old hole, sometimes beneath the earth's surface and sometimes above it, not infrequently in such unlikely locations as chimney flues, tops of pollarded trees and even more bizarre locations. Frequently, they inhabit old rabbit holes, which they enlarge to suit their convenience, but also they have been known to take up residence in a badger sett; indeed it is not uncommon for fox, badger and rabbit to live together in the same hole. This is where serious trouble can emerge, for to be discovered merely in the vicinity of a badger sett with a dog of any kind, with or without the landowner's permission to be there, is getting closer to the mark than most of us would wish to find ourselves, whilst for a terrier to enter such a sett, even should it do so under its own volition without any encouragement, is to expose its owner, and anyone with him, to the full weight of the law. Mark well, by the way, that a badger sett is interpreted in the Schedule to the Protection of Badgers Act 1992 as a structure or place which displays signs indicating that it is currently being used by a badger. This can mean a soil hole, a hole in a building, or a hole in a tree.

Badgers currently rank amongst some of the most rigorously protected species on this planet and are the subject of the Badgers Act 1973, The Badgers Act 1991, and the Badgers (Further Protection) Act 1991, all of which are consolidated under the Protection of Badgers Act 1992. Under this legislation it is unlawful to kill, injure or take, or attempt to kill, injure or take a badger. It is also an offence to have in one's possession a dead badger, or parts of a dead badger. There is a presumption that anyone found digging in or near a badger sett is digging for badger unless it can be shown to the contrary and this is for the accused to prove to the satisfaction of the Court. Should anyone be found in the act of committing any of these offences on any land, the owner or occupier of the land, or anyone employed by him, or a police officer may require the person committing the act to quit the land immediately and to give his name and address. Failure to comply in any respect will make him guilty of a further offence. So far, we have considered but one Section of the Act, which goes on for a further twelve Sections.

Section 2 deals with cruelty to badgers and covers the use of badger tongs and of firearms. Section 3 provides that anyone found damaging or destroying a badger sett or obstructing access to it or introducing a dog to it, is guilty of an offence, one to which it would be far from easy to provide an acceptable defence. The sale or possession of live badgers also constitute offences and are covered by Section 4 of the Act whilst, under the provisions of Section 5, any person, who rings or marks a badger without a Licence to do so, also finds himself foul of the law.

In further Sections of the Act, there is a provision for the taking of badgers under certain circumstances as in the case of injured animals or where danger to crops, livestock or buildings arises but, before any of these acts of mercy or conservation may be carried out, a Licence, which may or may not be granted by the appropriate Conservancy Council must be obtained, as must the permission of any landowner involved.

The penalties which may be incurred are severe. Section 12 of the Act provides for sentences of 6 months imprisonment or a £5,000 fine or both in respect of each offence. This is the maximum penalty should only one badger be involved and it should be borne in mind that the fines and jail sentences are calculated on a per badger basis. Thus, should a person be convicted of offences in respect of say four badgers (not an unusual number) in one sett, he could be looking at a £20,000 fine and two years imprisonment. For failure to quit land when so required under S.1(5) of the Act there is a maximum fine of £3,000.

Looking at reports of a few recent prosecutions under the Act, one forms the opinion that acquittals are few and, although fines were likely to be imposed in 1992 when this legislation came into force, nowadays a custodial sentence might be expected. So it will be seen that every precaution should be taken to ensure that, at very least, one's dog should be on a lead in the vicinity of anything which resembles a badger sett or in country with which one is not familiar.

So, you still want to have a go at fox. The first thing that you must obtain before so doing is the permission of the owner of the land. Make sure that this is in writing; word of mouth just is not sufficient. You may now be in a position to make a start.

Having reached the scene of operations, you may then set about getting on terms with your fox. But then spare a minute or so for a second thought. Are you quite certain that you are not putting your terrier into a badger sett? You know all the signs of badger occupation, the scratch marks on nearby trees, the badger latrines, those neat little holes dug into the ground and into which the creatures defecate, the huge amount of spoil which has been excavated.

There are several different ways of dealing with a fox once it has been bolted from below ground but there is but one way of pushing them out of their subterranean retreats and this is with the assistance of a terrier. Or maybe that is the wrong way of putting it; the terrier is the main participant in the matter and it may be helped, or for that matter hindered, by the human element and the lurcher or lurchers if these are being used. Should lurchers not be on the scene then the fox has to be taken in a net or else shot as soon as it puts in its appearance. I would say that a well set net should form part of the act whatever other means that you use, should the creature escape being netted. I am aware that some hunters go after fox with both guns and lurchers but I would advise against this unless you are absolutely confident that your dog will not run in at the critical moment.

Like every form of hunting, the quieter that you can be the more your efforts are likely to be attended with success and it is for this reason, if for no other, that I would prefer a terrier and lurcher combination rather than that of terrier and gun. As well as this reason for using a lurcher rather than a gun there is also another one and, should you be hunting on land other than your own, you will probably discover that whilst you may be quite welcome to carry out your pest control activities with the aid of dogs a very different view may be taken about the use of firearms. You may find that gamekeepers have rather uncompromising views about shooting on their preserves by persons other than themselves and their employers. Some of them maintain rather similar views concerning lurchers, in which case you may have to rely fairly heavily upon your ability to set a purse net.

In the same way as the rabbit hunting lurcher to ferrets, the fox hunting lurcher to terriers should be firmly discouraged from sniffing and snuffling around the earths. It must, of course, be encouraged to mark to earth and show you when a fox is present, but all the sound and fury in the act must be part of the underground scenario, that of the terrier. Whereas all hell can and should be created below ground everything on the surface should be as quiet as the grave, thus in its way perhaps seeming to reverse the natural order of things.

Make any noise or disturbance above ground and you will reap not your reward but the fruits of your actions in having to dig to your fox. You may have to do so in any case but there is little point in going out of your way to create for yourself a strenuous and boring chore. You will also by this means, that of leading the fox to bolt only as a matter of last resort, achieve very much less in the way of kills in the course of a day's work.

As I have said, it may be necessary to dig in any case for you cannot leave your terrier to ground on a fox which refuses to be dislodged, and so just make sure that you have a serviceable digging implement with you. Nothing in the way of ex-service entrenching tools, for although these are all very well as an emergency tool for digging to either terriers or ferrets, you will require something a good deal more robust than the infantryman's standby. A good pick and shovel are without doubt the best tools for the job. The best type of digging implement for the sportsman is a graft, the tool of the old time land drainers, with its narrow heavy blade and short wooden shaft. Do not forget to sharpen it before each occasion on which you take it out either; a suitably sharpened spade takes more than half the labour out of digging. However, let's hope that you do not need to use it too often. This will to a very great extent depend upon how much noise you and your lurcher create, or do not create above ground.

As to nets, you may prefer to construct your own or you may buy them ready made. There is not really very much difference between the two sorts in the way in which they perform, although there has to be a certain satisfaction in using anything which you have made yourself. The main thing is to set them properly and without a lot of hammering and banging around. For this reason a well sharpened elder peg takes a good deal of beating for pegging them down. Pegs of this material take a very sharp point enabling them to be pushed in by hand in all but the hardest and impermeable of soils. Added to this there is also the indisputable fact that these are the lightest pegs that you can have, which is a consideration of some importance where large numbers of nets have to be carried anywhere, although this is more likely to be the case when rabbiting than foxing.

Most lurchers will enter to fox without much fuss but there are some who, let's face it, are a bit short on bottle where this sort of quarry is concerned. With the right sort of terrier blood, preferably Airedale or Bedlington, there should not be too many problems of this kind. This sort of dog usually has the right sort of bite for dealing with fox. Like the catch as catch can wrestler of old a powerful grip coupled with a strong neck is what is required. I think that this is where disappointments can occur when collie blooded lurchers are tried against fox. A touch of Deerhound in the mixture is also very useful, for the working varieties of these dogs were the archetypal right hand helpmates of the Highland vermin controllers, the todhunters of old.

Train your lurcher to sit or lie down a little way back from the earth. That way he or she can get good all round vision and get away to a flying start on the fox, whatever unlikely spot it may emerge from. Some people work without nets and just rely upon one or two lurchers to deal with the quarry when it bolts. This has a good deal to recommend it, given the right sort of country, open hillsides and that sort of terrain where there is very little in the way of obstacles to hamper the pursuit, but in closer country you are likely to lose quite a few foxes that way. There is one great advantage, of course, in not using nets, that you will be making much less disturbance above ground and, therefore, your fox is more liable to make a run for it thus obviating the necessity for much in the way of digging.

LAMPING

The other way of taking fox, that is on the lamp, is a good method of dealing with them should you not have any friendly terriermen around and if you do not want to be bothered with keeping terriers yourself. As I have mentioned earlier, I am of the firm opinion that lurchers and terriers do not mix very well and many a promising running dog has been ruined by working it with a terrier. This does not apply to the same extent when hunting fox as it does when the quarry is rabbit for in the former instance, there is far less likelihood of disputed catches.

Lamping for foxes follows much the same sort of principles as apply to lamping for rabbits except, of course, you need a more aggressive and powerful lurcher than would be strictly necessary for rabbiting. Also foxes tend to get wise to the lamp and lampers rather faster and more effectively than do rabbits. For this reason, as in the case of lamping rabbits, it is advisable not to visit the same spot too frequently or too regularly.

A certain amount of 'salting' the ground, that is laying bait of some kind, will prove effective in attracting foxes to your scene of operations. There is nothing to beat a bit of hard weather for doing this. Any sort of carrion will do, the smellier the better. Rabbit guts, slaughterhouse waste, dead fowls, all of these and similar sorts of disgusting stuff are just about ideal.

I find that there is a good deal of satisfaction in taking foxes by any sort of method. They are unmitigated pests and the official foxhunts, apart from the footpacks of the North of England, and some of the better managed mounted packs, do little to curb their numbers. I have recently been hearing noises from a local foxhunt to the effect that, due to the

'Lamping for foxes follows much the same sort of principles as apply to lamping rabbits except, of course, you need a more aggressive and powerful Lurcher ...' Kevin Beaumont's Lurcher bitch, Abbey, with a large dog fox.

efforts of people with terriers and others with lurchers, there are so few foxes that they are thinking of giving up hunting. The only answer to that one is that I am quite sure that their absence from the sporting scene will not be noticed on account of the number of foxes which they take. Not much point their blaming those who are successful where they have failed, although it is always the way of the world to do so.

Feathered Quarry

There remains quarry of an entirely different kind from that which has so far been discussed and this is the feathered sort. One assumes that most people who engage in country activities may have heard the term, kanniechor, the Romany word meaning chicken thief and chicken thieving has been the purpose for which some lurchers have regrettably been kept in times now gone. In the present day, when most poultry are kept in battery houses, or on deep litter or under various fairly closely organised systems which go under the name of 'free range', the few hens which used to congregate around the back door of the farmhouse, scratching for a living in the now non-existent stackyard, are just as much bygones as the binder and the threshing machine and heavy horses and the steam traction engine. Another aspect of our lives in these days of factory farming being the availability of supermarket poultry meat at a price far lower than that which was charged in respect of what used to be the poor man's joint, neck end of mutton, also contributes to render the kanniechor likewise a thing of the past. This, though, has not always been so, and, in the days when the flesh of domestic fowl was esteemed as a quite expensive delicacy, poultry-stealing dogs existed. One of the first lurchers that I ever encountered was one of these animals and, as matters turned out, I was able to see the way it worked at first hand, not that, at the time, there was much satisfaction in that.

It was one of those golden days of summer going into autumn, of which, in retrospect, there seemed to be so many in those faraway days between the two world wars. I had just left school and was waiting to commence the next stage in the development of what, at that time, appeared to be my future career – as it happened things turned out rather differently, but that's another story and half the world away. Normally, there would have been some job to do around the farm, but we had arrived at one of the comparatively slack times of the year; the corn had been carried with the stooks gone from the fields, and potato gathering was three weeks ahead. So, not being an expert rick thatcher, I had managed to absent myself for the day, giving as an excuse that I wished to visit some distant cousins on the other side of the river.

On my way, I had to pass over the Stainforth and Keadby canal where I saw, leaning on the bridge, an acquaintance of mine, Ben by name. He was engaged in conversation with two men on a barge, which was in the lock just beneath him; the discussion, which was carried out in shouts, was of a desultory nature and I had no difficulty in joining in. The state of the tide in the river outside was not quite right for them to proceed down the Trent and Humber to Hull, or so they said, and, as they cleared the lock, it was proposed that we adjourned to the neighbouring public house, that grand old canalside inn, The Friendship, for a pint or two to pass the time, which was something of which we all seemed to possess a fair amount that morning.

'Fetch the dog wi'thee,' said one of the crewmen to the other, at which his companion gave a whistle and from somewhere aboard the boat there came what, at first, appeared to be a collie of some kind. As it leapt easily on to the quayside, it was apparent that it was rather longer in the leg and back than the average sheepdog and had a bit more than pure sheepdog blood in it. We all went into the pub, the dog accompanying us. I purchased four pints of Barnsley Bitter and carried them over to the table where the other three had seated themselves. By now the subject of conversation had turned to dogs.

'Aye, he's a right champion sort,' one of the men was saying, 'Catch owt. Rabbits, hares, owt.'

I regarded this reputed paragon of the canine species which had by now disposed itself in front of the empty fireplace. 'Doesn't look as though it would have the speed,' I ventured. In those days I was beginning to regard myself as becoming something of an expert in such matters, for had I not been exercising the headmaster's chauffeur's whippet on Saturday afternoons in my last year at the old school?

The man whom I addressed regarded me with apparent surprise and disbelief. 'Don't know how you can reckon that,' he said. 'He's by Waterloo Cup winner year afore last.'

By now, the pint pots of our two new acquaintances were empty and Ben went to the bar and bought in another round. I had not continued the conversation by entering into another argument with the chap, who looked just the type with whom it might be imprudent to too readily disagree.

We continued to contemplate the animal in silence, meanwhile each with, no doubt, his separate and differing opinions of it – or maybe not.

He was the first to speak after a long and deliberate pull at his beer. 'Tell you what I'll do. You seem to be a right sort of lad even if you don't know a good half bred grew when you see one. So I'll give him to thee and thoo can try him for theesen.'

Their beer pots once more being empty, I wondered if he or his companion would further extend their generosity by purchasing a refill but my mind was quickly set at rest on that score. 'Time we was off.

Tide's rising,' said the other man as they both made for the door. The dog seemed to have settled itself and made no attempt to follow them.

Ben and I looked at one another. 'Well, we got that one for nowt,' said he. 'Can't be so bad. We'd better try him. Let's take him down to Bullhassocks; there's plenty of rabbits sitting out there now that the corn's cut.'

Bullhassocks was an ill drained field of rough grass such as would never be seen today, such pasturage very rightly having been one of the first casualties of the War Agricultural Executive Committee's intensive plough-up policies in 1939. Permanent grassland, like this, served some sort of purpose, however. At a rental of maybe five or ten shillings an acre, it fed a few bullocks during the summer and its tussocky clumps of rushes and coarse grasses provided a useful haven for snipe and hare in their season and, in the warmer months, could be relied upon to provide a bolting rabbit or two for the gun. It was a couple of miles or so away and we set off to walk there, the dog at our heels.

As we arrived at the gate of the field and started to untie the binder twine with which it was secured, the farmer hove into view from the opposite direction. 'Going to give the old dog a try?' he enquired. 'There's plenty of rabbits in there now. Just leave us a couple, if you get any, and you're welcome to the rest.' He departed down the lane as we entered the field.

Before we had gone twenty yards, a rabbit shot up at our feet. The dog paid no regard despite our enthusiastically urging it on. Towards the middle of the field, the same thing occurred with the dog taking as little interest as it had on the previous occasion, and so it went on and on and on. I had never known the field so full of rabbits sitting out in the rough grass but the dog displayed not the slightest interest in any of them. We soon decided that we had had enough and dispiritedly prepared to return to the village. As we made our way back along the lane, the dog followed us, staying a few feet behind.

'Not much use, is it?' Ben put into words what was going through the minds of both of us.

'No,' I agreed. 'It isn't. What do we do with it now?'

'I'll keep it for a bit. It seems friendly enough and might make a bit of a pet for the kids.' He was some years older than I was and, as well as being a married man, had two young children.

As he was speaking, we were about a hundred yards short of an outlying farmstead and, as I looked behind me, I realised that the dog was no longer with us.

'Where's it gone,' I wondered.

'Maybe taken itself off and we've lost it,' Ben said hopefully. After looking over the hedges and whistling to no avail, we continued on our way. By now, we were a quarter of a mile beyond the farm buildings.

'Maybe it'll find us,' said Ben and words were never more rapidly proved to be correct for, out of the shadow of the hedgerow, appeared the dog, a plump hen in its mouth. It preferred the bird to Ben, who automatically took hold of it. It was apparent that the fowl was unharmed and very much alive, so alive, in fact that its recipient dropped it, whereupon it fled squawking through the hedge and into the field, where, from the noises it was making, it was in good fettle and making its way back home with no delay. The dog made no attempt to follow it but instead took up station immediately behind us. When we reached Ben's cottage, we prepared to go our separate ways, he with the dog in tow. I did not see him for another week.

'Where's the dog? What's happened to it?' I immediately enquired.

'Don't rightly know. It just took itself off a couple of days back and I haven't seen it since.'

We adjourned to The Friendship for a pint. As he drew the beer, the landlord remarked, 'Had those two mates of yours in day before yesterday, those chaps off the barge. They had the old dog with them.'

And that is the account of how temporary board and lodging was given to a kanniechor whilst its owners no doubt sampled the fleshpots of Hull. There must be a moral to such a tale, something like, 'always look a gift horse in the mouth,' but I think perhaps the words of the immortal Jorrocks better fit the bill. 'Confound all gifts,' I sez, 'Wot eats!'

This all happened some sixty years ago and the conditions for such dogs to be worth keeping by someone, who let's face it, is neither more nor less than a thief, no longer exist. It crosses one's mind, however, that the sort of dog which can effectively and silently pick up a live chicken might also be capable of dealing in a similar way with a live pheasant or a partridge. I always suspected, as did the Normanby Park gamekeepers, that the dog which I described at the beginning of this book was one such creature, and I would not like to take my oath on there not being a few animals with similar aptitudes still in existence. So game preservers, beware.

— 9 —
Grief And How To Avoid It

LIVESTOCK

The biggest problem is livestock in general and sheep in particular. Sheep are knot-headed, foolish animals and I should know for I used to run some 4,000 of them.

Sadly, though, it is not merely a matter of the knotheadedness and imbecility of the beasts which we have to worry about, although these are bad enough in themselves. One fact which will become abundantly obvious to you, once you are the proud owner of a lurcher or longdog, is that whether you be duke or dustman, you will be viewed with suspicion by the vast majority of farmers, who will now look upon you as a potential menace not only to game but also to their sheep. The farmer, who yesterday was pleased to make your acquaintance as you had a good terrier or two with which you might be relied upon to reduce his rat population, will henceforth regard you with disfavour as the owner of a possible livestock worrier.

You will meet the owners of lurchers who will state, quite truthfully, that their dogs will course a hare through a flock of sheep and will not touch any of them. Indeed most of us who have trained our dogs in the correct way will be able to say this. But unless you know the owner of the sheep very well and, moreover, have a complete understanding with him

155

on the matter, I would not advise anyone to try doing this. The presence of a dog of any kind but more particularly a running dog, even in an adjacent field, is likely to give rise to paroxysms of passion of the most unrestrained nature. Bear in mind also that, should you and your dog be in the same field as livestock and it is not under absolute control, which most magistrates in rural areas will unhesitatingly interpret as being on a lead, you will be in breach of the law. Should your dog give chase to anything through a flock of sheep, this will unfailingly be construed as your dog having chased sheep. So be warned; dogs and sheep can be bad news.

Should livestock actually be attacked then it at once becomes a case of double, double toil and trouble. In the first place you will be nailed for letting your dog carry out the dreaded act and this will almost always result in a conviction coupled with a heavy fine.

But this is not the end of the matter. Having pawned all the family heirlooms in order to pay your fines and legal expenses, you may be excused for relaxing for a moment and for drawing a sigh of relief that all is over. Do not allow yourself to be complacent, however, for, as night follows day, you may soon look forward to a knock on your door and to receive a summons to appear before the civil court to show cause why you should not pay something astronomical in the way of damages to the owner of the livestock which has suffered at the jaws of your dog. Since you have already been convicted in the criminal court you will not have very much in the way of a defence and so probably will decide that rather than incur further heavy legal expenditure you will pay up and hope that this is the end of the matter. In addition to the financial penalties you and your family will also have suffered a good deal of anxiety and mental hassle and distress. If you have a shotgun certificate you may look forward to, on conviction, this being withdrawn or almost certainly not being renewed.

BADGERS

If livestock, particularly sheep are the most frequent source of trouble to those who work their lurchers, then the badger is probably the animal, any involvement with which, can lead to disastrous consequences. The badger is a creature to be avoided at all costs, and should any of the lurcher or terrier owners, whom I know, find themselves anywhere, where there is the slightest sign of badgers being present, will immediately quit the locality and, henceforth, give it an extremely wide berth. What was at one time regarded by most country people as a fairly harmless wild animal which kept itself to itself, it was looked upon by others as something of a pest, particularly on the odd occasions when it undermined large areas of ground sometimes with spectacular results; I recollect one such occasion in the early 1930s when, in a field of corn, a binder was let down complete with horses.

No one that I have ever known, however, has wished them serious ill. Such sentiments, or rather lack of them, was for the criminal fringe whose lives were so small and horizons so limited that they derived some sort of entertainment from badger baiting, which, as a pastime, ranks with dog fighting and cat coursing. One wonders whether, perhaps, this sort of attitude was perhaps encouraged or, at any rate, made seem less reprehensible by the wholesale, and, to my mind, unnecessary, gassing of the creatures in the name of disease control in those instances where they have been blamed for the spread of diseases in cattle. Whatever the rights and wrongs of the latter, and it is not within the scope of this book to examine the situation, the law, as it stood regarding badgers was not judged sufficient to cope with what sometimes went on, hence the current legislation, the existence of which it is vitally important to keep at the forefront of one's mind, even when merely enjoying a country stroll accompanied by a dog of any sort.

DEER

Most species of deer are on the increase and are spreading geographically into areas where they have not previously been seen for many years. The taking of deer with the use of dogs is totally illegal in Scotland, whereas such is not entirely the case in other parts of the kingdom, where deer may not be taken except during the hours of daylight. This renders any form of taking them anywhere at night completely unlawful. It is, of course, also against the law to disturb them during any prescribed close season. The hunting of deer with lurchers or longdogs, even where and when it may not be strictly illegal, is far from advisable. It could scarcely be other than a very messy business with not only the probability of both hunter and dogs being exposed to serious injury, but also the even greater likelihood of his very properly being prosecuted for inflicting unnecessary suffering on the deer, the dog, or both.

In any case, it is exceedingly unlikely that any owner or occupier of land would grant permission for deer to be coursed on his land and any taking of deer without permission would, of course, be poaching and, on this score alone, completely illegal. For this type of activity the penalties are very severe indeed and, moreover, in most cases would also be accompanied by the prescribed seizure of any dogs or vehicles which may have been used.

PERMISSION

No matter what the quarry you should always ensure that you have the **written** permission of whoever has the right to take the game by virtue of ownership either of the land or of the sporting rights over it and do not forget that *all* land including common land in the United Kingdom belongs to someone. Make absolutely sure that the authority is in writing and is properly signed and dated. Verbal assent, apart from being easily rescinded, is not enough to satisfy the legal requirement. Should you be intending to do any lamping make sure that the words 'at all times' or 'during the hours of darkness' are included. With this on your person at all times you may sally forth with a certain amount of confidence, although it is just as well to bear in mind the necessity not to cause unnecessary pain and suffering to any animal in the course of your hunting activities.

OFFENSIVE WEAPONS

There are some people who, even should they merely be venturing into the garden with an airgun, seem unable to resist the urge to strap a sheath knife to themselves. It must be the Robin Hood or Davy Crockett which persists in some individuals. If you are working a lurcher, there is no necessity for such implements and, if possessed, are best left at home. A pocket knife with a blade of less than three inches will be quite sufficient for coupling and paunching any rabbits that you catch and will, in fact, prove to be a good deal handier to use. For that matter, why not learn the old gamekeeper's trick of using the rabbit's teeth rather than a knife, when coupling them.

Offensive weapons can also include sticks, particularly should they be a trifle heavier than might be necessary, and although a good ashplant can make an excellent substitute for a third leg, it is as well to consider the interpretation which, under certain circumstances, may be put upon carrying such an item.

Firearms, even if your certificate is in order and you have permission to use them, are best left in your gun safe unless you are specifically shooting game and using your lurcher in the role of setter or retriever.

It must never be forgotten that opposition to field sports in all their various forms is very well organised and funded and that, as well as those who are motivated purely by their consciences in the matter, there is a small minority who look upon it as a heaven-sent opportunity to further their political views. It is therefore imperative that we always carry out whatever we are doing strictly within the framework of the law and never furnish any of those who would seek to criticise us with the least excuse to do so.

Should you feel, however, that there are large numbers of persons ranged against field sports, take heart from one thing and that is that quite a number of the animal rights protesters, including some of those who seem violently opposed to field sports, frequently appear to be accompanied by lurchers, and one likes to think that anyone who favours lurchers cannot be all that bad.

THE ACTS OF PARLIAMENT

In connection with poaching the law is a trifle complicated, different Acts most of which are of archaic origin, being applicable depending upon the circumstances of each individual offence. The main laws on the subject were drafted in the early part of the nineteenth century when, as a result of the end of hostilities between the United Kingdom and the France of Napoleon a fair number of able bodied men well versed in the use of firearms were suddenly let loose upon the country. The Industrial Revolution with its mass migrations of workpeople from country to town was soon to follow and a certain amount of lawlessness was believed to be in the offing. Until then the game laws had been in an even bigger muddle, game only being able to be legally taken by qualified shots whose qualification rested not on proficiency with firearms but upon the ownership of land of a certain value. The effect of this had been that the man who owned a large amount of land was able to shoot over the property of anyone who had an acreage which was less than the qualifying size. All was very mixed up and very confusing. In fact something was done about it, the laws then enacted being with us still although with certain amendments, one of which is that the poacher is no longer sentenced to transportation for the third offence against the Night Poaching Act of 1828, so that there is little chance of getting an assisted passage to the Antipodes by this method any longer.

Most of the rest of the Night Poaching Act, 1828, is still in force, however, and anyone who is convicted of by night unlawfully entering or being upon land whether open or enclosed with any gun, net or other engine for taking or destroying game, faces a maximum fine of £200. Should he offer violence with an offensive weapon the fine is increased to £500 or six months imprisonment or both. Similar penalties may be enforced in those cases where three or more persons are together involved in committing the offence.

For poaching by day the penalties are less severe with a fine of £20 plus costs for entering on to land or being without leave on any land in search or pursuit of game including rabbits. If five or more people together trespass in search of game by day each is liable to a fine of £50 with costs with a further £25 fine if violence is used. The Game Act, 1831, also provides that if a person found on land in pursuit of game without permission refuses to give his name and address when required to do so by the occupier of the land or by his gamekeeper or servant, he may be arrested. For the purposes of the foregoing legislation daytime is defined as commencing at the beginning of the last hour before sunrise and concluding at the expiration of the first hour after sunset.

The trespasser in pursuit of game may also discover that he is in trouble under the Game Licences Act of 1860 under the provisions of which a game licence is not required for hunting rabbits with the permission of the occupier of the land but is required if poaching, such licence not being required at all if hares are being hunted.

Life for the poacher is made even more difficult by virtue of the Poaching Prevention Act, 1862, which gives the police the right to search persons or vehicles in a public place if they reasonably suspect that a poaching offence has taken place. Game, guns and other equipment may be seized but the offender may not be arrested on the spot. The penalty if convicted can be a fine of £50 and confiscation of the items which have been seized.

The person convicted under the Deer Act, 1963, of unlawfully coursing deer will find himself in even worse straits with a fine of £500 and possible confiscation of his vehicle. For being in illegal possession of venison the fine is likewise £500.

So, although you are no longer liable to find yourself being transported or doing a stint on the treadmill, the penalties are still severe. I hope that this is not going to put you off hunting altogether. My remarks are not intended to have this effect but only to indicate the very real pitfalls which exist. It is still possible to enjoy a day's coursing or a night's lamping without officious interference but one should never forget that the current attitude of many of the public towards any form of hunting is a very different one from that which prevailed only a few years ago. Due to the activities of various pressure groups, many of them with political motives, this is a frame of mind which is continually being fostered to the detriment of all field sportsmen so that we should always be seen to be doing things strictly according to the letter of the law.

— 10 —
Breeding Lurchers

Elsewhere in this book I have endeavoured to indicate a few of the pitfalls which are to be encountered in the course of the acquisition of a lurcher. If buying one is so hazardous why not breed one's own lurcher? In this way one might be certain of the pedigree of both the parents and so avoid the unpleasant surprises detailed earlier as the young dog begins to get its growth and starts to become a lurcher proper.

Well, that may be one way of looking at it. On the other hand, should you seriously be contemplating breeding, certain of the more obvious drawbacks to doing this should be evident. Are there suitable whelping quarters readily available? Have you any idea just how you are going to dispose of those of the litter which are surplus to your own requirements? Have you any idea of the breeding costs? If you have formed any opinion about these costs then I would advise you to take whatever figure has resulted from your calculations and double it. If you are a natural optimist and there must be a few about for the bankruptcy courts are full of them, then treble it. These are but a few of the snags which you are likely to encounter.

THE STUD DOG

However, if you are firmly intent upon breeding, if you have the right sort of stock available to do it and if you have a limitless supply of funds to finance the operation, then at least do things the right way. To start at the beginning you are going to need the services of a stud dog. Perhaps you already have a suitable dog yourself. It is the apple of your eye and all those whom you meet have intimated that, should it ever sire any pups, then they would insist upon having one of them. But before we go any further with this one, just what is the breeding behind this paragon of all things canine – which well it may be? What recessive factors are lurking there just waiting to be liberated by their fellows in the bitch's genetic makeup?

Unless you are completely sure of the breeding behind the dog (and in my opinion a lurcher sire should never be of any breeding more complex than the half bred) then look elsewhere. Similar considerations apply if you are going outside your own kennel in your selection of a stud dog. Were I to be seeking a stud dog for use on any sort of lurcher bitch I would most definitely hesitate before employing anything of other than sighthound blood, for example a pure bred Greyhound, Whippet or Deerhound or any cross between them. Should my brood bitch be of pure and unadulterated sighthound blood, again namely Greyhound, Whippet, Deerhound or any cross between these, I might select a half bred dog of the kind towards which I wished to breed. It all depends of course, upon the result which you seek to achieve at the end of the day.

INBREEDING, LINEBREEDING AND OUTCROSSING

It may be that your prospective sire and dam are related, in other words that you are going to inbreed. The advisability of doing this depends on how good a stockman and how good a geneticist you are. Again this is something which I would avoid where breeding animals of very mixed blood is concerned if for no other reason than that of not wishing to perpetuate a line of mongrels. However, even using animals of relatively uncomplicated breeding one is apt to produce some unexpected results when lurcher breeding, which is not at all the same game as breeding pure. For instance, if breeding two closely related animals of mixed Greyhound and terrier blood, the resultant litter might be expected to contain pups which, when grown, would be indistinguishable from purebred Greyhounds and terriers. This can occur with unrelated animals but you are really shortening the odds when inbreeding. It is an old adage of stockmen, 'Breed close and cull hard'. If you try linebreeding lurchers then ten to one if you are any sort of stockman, you will find yourself culling the lot, perhaps even including the breeding stock and yourself as well.

THE BITCH'S SEASON

So by now you know which way you are going, your dam and sire are selected for better or worse and all that needs to be done is to get on with it. For this you will have to wait until your bitch comes on heat. Various authorities on breeding will tell you all about this state of affairs commencing with a blood discharge, swollen vulva and so on, all of which you may never notice for quite a few longdog bitches are adept at not making much of a show of all this. Skittish behaviour and a disinclination to respond to commands should put you on alert and the signs may be there if you look for them, but it is still not all that easy to be exact as to the length of time that the bitch has been showing colour. Calculating from the first day of heat you will be advised to put your bitch to the dog at the eleventh day. Do not be too cast down if nothing occurs on this occasion. Most tyro breeders are, I find, inclined to be a bit previous at this stage of the proceedings.

Amongst Greyhound breeders it is usually reckoned that the best time for the bitch to go to the dog is between the thirteenth and eighteenth days from when the bitch came on heat, the first day upon which she began to show colour. The optimum day for mating may vary according to various more or less imponderable factors such as her age, how many litters she may have had and so on. This is very much a case of 'if at first you don't succeed, try, try again' and whatever you do, do not give up for the reason that at their first encounter the dog and bitch do not make it. Owners and stud grooms of dogs which are regularly used are very knowledgeable about these matters and eager to help. I always considered that taking a bitch to the late and very much lamented Bob Whitehead for service by one of his dogs was more instructive than a veterinary course in the subject.

THE MATING

If you are not taking your bitch to a stud which is regularly used, things can sometimes be a bit perplexing so that should you and some inexperienced acquaintance be engaged in the proceedings, there are one or two things which you should bear in mind. The bitch should be muzzled for a start as things can sometimes get a bit hectic and it is as well that all precautions are taken against any injury to the stud dog, or indeed to yourself. Let the two dogs play around for a while in a paddock or other enclosed space. This will usually result in mating taking place but, should it not, you may have to try again on the following day. Time will usually be found to be on your side on such occasions. Some young bitches may prove a bit skittish and have to be held in place for the dog to mount.

When the mating does take place, the participants will become 'tied' or in other words locked together, this being caused by the swelling of the sexual organs to the extent that withdrawal becomes impossible. After service the dog will usually dismount by cocking his hind leg over the bitch's back so that they will remain tied in a back to back posture. It is of the greatest importance at this stage that both animals, but the bitch in particular, should be restrained otherwise injury may result. For this reason never less than two persons should be present when a mating takes place. Some virgin bitches may be found to be a bit constricted in the vagina and mating will obviously be difficult, in which case a little vaseline often works wonders but if this fails, a visit to the vet for a very minor operation may be necessary. The various sorts of longdog seem more prone to this difficulty than do most other breeds.

After mating, both dog and bitch should be rested. Do not go for a second service on the same day as would be the case with the larger domestic animals. However, there is no reason why you should not try for a second mating on the following or a subsequent day and most longdog breeders are firmly of the opinion that not only is this the way to ensure satisfactory mating but also that larger litters will be produced. This is not without scientific confirmation.

THE BITCH IN WHELP

Assuming that all has gone to plan, the pregnant bitch will be in whelp for a period of 63 days. In the case of lurcher bitches, they usually deliver the goods on time but may occasionally be a day or two early or late. The bitch should have been drenched for round worm before mating and she should be given a second dose at the end of the second week of pregnancy. Apart from this life should go on much as normal. You may find the bitch going off her food a few weeks after mating but this is nothing to worry about unless it persists unduly and is usually a fairly sure sign that she has 'clicked' and is in whelp. Exercise her regularly and feed as normal. Do not overfeed.

WHELPING QUARTERS

Nothing over elaborate is required in the way of whelping quarters and upon more than one occasion, despite my having made whelping boxes of the most comprehensive kind, complete with guard rails to ensure that the pups are not overlaid and so on, bitches have frustrated my intentions and produced litters on my bedroom floor or on the landing outside. Personally, I feel that at a time like this the bitch is apt to know best and have left it to them even to the extent that they have retired down aardvark holes to have their litters when I lived in Africa. Somewhere close at hand is obviously the best and as long as there is a plentiful supply of bedding in the form of old newspaper to absorb the mess, very little in the way of harm is likely to result. I am not, of course, referring to breeding on anything like a commercial scale when purpose built quarters to meet the requirements of the local Environmental Health authorities would be necessary.

Makeshift quarters, however, whilst quite suitable for whelping, will not do for long in the face of a growing litter and after the first couple of weeks a place with more space and facilities for being regularly cleansed will be necessary. Any sort of outhouse, as long as it is wind and weatherproof will do, provided it is sufficiently spacious and has some room outside where the pups will be able to run around. The size of the bitch will have a bearing on the matter of course, as will the size of the litter, something in the nature of a Whippet requiring less space than a Deerhound. Cold weather whelpings are not recommended except in the case of commercial breeders, who will have to be properly equipped and should not require any of my advice anyway, but should these take place, some form of heating will be necessary if the litter is to thrive or indeed survive. Whatever accommodation is chosen for the bitch and litter one of the basic requirements is some sort of a bench in order that the bitch can get off the floor well away from what will become the ever increasing demands of the pups.

As soon as you are certain that your dog is in whelp it is advisable that you should consult your veterinary surgeon who will advise you as to worming, inoculations and so on. He or she should also be informed as to the estimated date of whelping so that, should anything go wrong, he will be in the picture even if only to a minimal extent.

WHELPING

All should by now be ready for whelping to take place and on or about the 63rd day your bitch will show signs of this being imminent. If you fancy being terribly scientific about it or if you are just naturally an anxious sort, you can be given very positive indication of this by taking her temperature at regular twice daily intervals starting 10 days before you expect parturition to take place. Temperatures, as in all animals, are taken rectally and it will be found that between 12 and 24 hours prior to the actual whelping your bitch's temperature will drop from the normal 101.4° Fahrenheit down to about 99°F. In any case, a few hours before whelping she will develop bouts of uneasiness interspersed with lying stretched out, meanwhile giving you dirty looks which after all are fairly justified, you being the author of all the trouble. She will do a good bit of licking of the area beneath her tail and may be off her food. She may well endeavour to dig a hole in the floor or the seat of your favourite settee at this stage so that, for this reason, if for no other, it is essential that she should not be left on her own.

As soon as she begins to push and strain at intervals varying this with a fair bit of digging and tearing at her bed you will know that things are well under way. She can be left to get on with things herself but if this stage should be prolonged for anything over about three hours, call the vet.

The first thing to appear will not be a pup but the water sac. This may break of its own accord or, if not, will be broken by the bitch licking it after which the first pup should put in its appearance. If it should appear to be necessary to do so, clear the membrane away from its nose and hold it head down to clear its nostrils and throat. Should the pup appear to be jammed in the birth canal you can give it a bit of help, grasping it with a bit of rough towelling and easing it out in time with the bitch's contractions. Don't pull when the bitch is not contracting and don't twist the pup in any way or you will probably break its neck. When you pull, if you have to do so, pull down and in the direction of the bitch's head, not straight or towards her tail.

Breech presentations are common but are not attended with the same sort of difficulties as are such presentations in other forms of animal life. There is, however, a possibility of the whelp being drawn back inside, where it may suffocate, so gently get it away if matters seem to be taking too long. The pup should be followed by the placenta or afterbirth which the bitch will probably try to devour. There are two schools of thought about this. The back to nature faction believe that valuable properties are contained in the placenta and that consuming it will contribute to the dam's wellbeing; the hygienic contingent feel that all placentas should be removed for subsequent destruction. Being of a fairly open mind about the matter myself, I do not have any strong feelings in either direction and do whatever is convenient. The only difference seems to be that, should the bitch eat the afterbirths, she will be a bit loose in the bowels and scour the following day. The main thing to remember is to account for all the placentas which should be presented at the rate of one per pup. Should any be missing, the most likely absentee being the last one, send for the vet. In any case it is not a bad plan particularly if this is your first whelping, to let him check your bitch over 24 hours after parturition has taken place.

Make sure that all the pups find the food supply and retrieve any which get underneath or at the back of their mother. Personally, I weigh all pups at birth and thereafter at weekly intervals until they become too big. This is by no means an absolute necessity but I find it a useful aid to checking the progress of the litter and of observing which pup is doing what. By now you will probably be wondering whatever it was that led you to go in for dog breeding and swearing never to embark upon such a project ever again. Go and take a well earned rest and leave your bitch to it; she will be all the better for being left on her own for a bit. Give her and the litter plenty of privacy for the following week. Resist the efforts of acquaintances and small children to have just a quick look at the dear little puppies; the time for this will come later when all of them will be more than welcome as part of the socialising process.

DEWCLAWS

Two other matters should engage your attention for the moment. One of these is the removal of dewclaws. It is more than likely that they will prove to be a nuisance if left on any sort of running dog and the best time to remove them is during the first day or so of a pup's life. This was one of those minor operations which were carried out by most breeders but which is now, inadvisedly to my mind, a matter for the attention of a vet.

Under the provisions of Statutory Instrument 1412 of 1991, The Veterinary Surgeons Act 1966 (Schedule 3 Amendment) Order 1991, any docking of a dog's tail or removal of its dewclaws by other than a qualified person was prohibited as from July 1, 1993.

This prohibition has also been enacted under Article 10 of The European Convention for the Protection of Pet Animals, which not only covers tail docking and dewclaw removal but also ear cropping, devocalisation, defanging and emasculation.

So, if you want your pup's dewclaws removed, and I would strongly advise you to have it done, you will require the services of a veterinary surgeon.

Depending on the vet, of course, you may also have to convince him of the necessity for the operation.

CULLING

The other consideration is that of just how many of the litter you wish to keep. Any which are not in every way perfect should be put down and a good deal of thought should be given as to which of the remainder should be allowed to survive. It is a rotten decision to have to make but will save untold heartache at some later stage when the pups have turned into individuals, all of whom you will know well by this time. Today's market for lurchers is not a buoyant one and dog puppies will frequently be found not to sell so that there is a fairly good case for destroying all the dogs in a litter unless, of course, you have definite orders for such, or if the litter should consist preponderantly of dogs. Even in the latter case I should still be inclined to think twice. At this stage you will once again wonder what on earth impelled you to take up breeding.

CARE OF THE BITCH AND PUPPIES

From now on the bitch's rations should be increased and since a good deal of demand is being put upon her system it is not a bad idea to feed her three meals consisting of at least two pounds of meat with a biscuit supplement, per day. She will not want to leave the pups for long but should be encouraged to take short trips outside to relieve herself at intervals. Meanwhile bedding can be changed and the youngsters can be subjected to a bit closer examination than when she is present, since it is best to do nothing to cause her the least anxiety. Keep an eye on her when she is getting in and out of her bed and try to keep her from treading on any of the pups.

By the time that the first week has elapsed the bitch will be ready to leave the pups for somewhat longer periods and can be taken for short walks for anything up to about half an hour. She should also be getting over the messy stage so that an old blanket may be substituted for the waste paper bedding. Do not use anything in which the pups can become entangled as they are quite good at doing this sort of thing during the first couple of weeks or so of their lives. The bitch will clean up after the pups but it is as well to give her every assistance in the shape of frequent clean bedding.

At the age of between 10 and 14 days the puppies' eyes will begin to open. Should they show any signs of resealing, wipe them clean with a piece of damp cotton wool so as to keep any infection out. Avoid bright light; this may adversely effect their eyesight. In Victorian times the human infants in remote country areas of Britain were not permitted to see daylight until they were six weeks of age. My father was treated thus as a baby and perhaps as a consequence, did not require spectacles until he had turned eighty. The hearing of the puppies is also beginning to function at this time and they will begin to take notice albeit to a minimal degree, of their surroundings.

WEANING

A week after their eyes have opened it is time to start them on supplementary feeding in the shape of semi-solid food. There are several proprietary puppy foods on the market but these tend to be expensive and expense is something of which you will be having more than your fair share round about now. In my experience they do just as well on oatmeal and milk sweetened with some honey. Dip their noses in it and leave them to lick it off when they will soon get the idea and start to lap. Get them on to meat as well, given to them in the form of scraped meat. This is quite easily prepared; just get hold of a piece of lean beef and scrape the surface of it with a sharp knife so that the pulp is scraped off to leave the fibrous part of the meat behind. The pups are fed the pulp and the dam the fibrous remainder. The litter should be fed little and often at this stage, four or five meals a day being about right.

As time goes on food should become of a more solid nature and by the fourth week the litter can be taking well minced tripe and puppy meal soaked in gravy. Keep them to five meals a day spread as widely through the 24 hours as you can without doing anything extreme like getting up in the middle of the night to give them a feed.

SOCIALISING

By this time the pups will have become very lively and playful and should be getting outside into the fresh air for a good part of their time. Now is the time to start socialising them and the more time that you can spend with them the better. If you have young children eager to play with them, this is just about an ideal situation which will pay off for the rest of the pups' lives as well as making the job of training them that bit easier.

WORMING

The litter should have its first worming about now. This will be for round worm and should be repeated at about six weeks of age. It will then be possible to state that any puppies which you sell, have been recently wormed; this should be an added selling point as well as having the effect of dissuading purchasers from trying out any patent nostrums of their own such as tobacco or powdered glass. The state of all medication progresses at such a rate that I do not intend to recommend any particular variety of worming medicine, but would advise you to obtain this from your vet who will have the most up-to-date and efficient available.

SELLING THE PUPPIES

The pups will be ready to leave their mother by the time that they are six weeks old and should any sensible and responsible lurcher person who is known to you as such, wish to purchase a puppy, then let it go. I should be rather more wary of a person whom I did not know or who was not vouched for by someone I knew, although in general conversation it should be possible to get some idea of whether or not a prospective purchaser knows what he or she is about. By the time that the puppies are eight weeks old is the ideal age at which they should be taken off your hands. With this in mind do not forget to get your advertisements off to press in good time. *The Countryman's Weekly* is a good media for advertising lurchers but will require at least four weeks before being able to get anything into print. When submitting your advertising matter inform them as to which issue you would like to see it appear in. In your advertisement give your telephone number and also your general geographical location. The latter will be helpful to prospective purchasers in making up their minds about what distance it is sensible to go for their requirements. Most buyers come along in person in these days of almost universal road travel but very occasionally you may be asked to send a pup over a long distance and the best way of doing this still seems to be by rail.

Selling a litter of lurcher pups can be a very interesting experience and in the course of your marketing and sales activities it is quite likely that you will make the acquaintance of some very strange characters indeed. Naturally you will want to see your puppies going off to good homes and will do your best to ensure that this takes place although at the same time you will be anxious to get those which you have earmarked for sale, off your hands as soon as possible for by now not only will they be becoming a pretty boisterous lot but they will also be costing you an arm and a leg in food.

Do not be over anxious to sell at this point, however, for with all pups in general it is possible for them to get to other than good homes. As far as lurchers are concerned this is if anything, more likely to occur. Just as the world of fast horses has always had a fringe of undesirables, so has the world of sporting dogs. This is where you may find that it has paid off for you to have visited a few lurcher shows and to have kept your eyes and ears open whilst you have been there so as to weigh up the form of potential owners a bit.

You will, of course, expect to discuss with a prospective purchaser the type of home in which the pup which you are selling is likely to wind up but it is a wicked world and there are far too many of those about who are only too ready to tell us what they imagine we should like to hear without overmuch regard for the truth. The purchasers whom I most welcome are first and foremost, people whom I know and who have had experience of owning a dog of some sort previously. It is all to the good if at least one member of the family is not working so that they are able to be at home a good bit of the time and to give the dog the attention it deserves.

Couples out at work for a good part of the day are frequently the cause of trouble with young dogs which become lonely and bored, frequently venting their feelings to the detriment of the interior furnishings. The dog is punished for this, not knowing why it is being dealt with in this harsh manner. Sometimes it is banished to unsuitable quarters and sometimes turned out to roam the streets.

Prospective owners who are not sound in wind and limb are not much use either, for a person needs to be in possession of all his faculties in order to give a lurcher the amount of exercise which is necessary for its wellbeing. On the whole this can be a very difficult time and one during which decisions do not come easily. The market in lurchers is not anything like it used to be, when there was plenty of free publicity given annually by the media at the time of the Lambourn Lurcher Show, alas by now nothing more than a part of lurcher history. It is more than likely that you will have a good part of the litter left some weeks after they have left their mother and they will be eating you out of house and home. Gone will be any idea of the road to swift riches and yet again you will wonder what on earth prompted you to take up lurcher breeding.

INOCULATION

Time now for yet more of these irksome decisions for by the time the pups are 10 weeks old you will have to think about having them inoculated against the killer diseases of Distemper, Parvovirus and Leptospirosis. This will be given in two doses, the first at 10 weeks old and the second a month later. Until they have had the second dose, in order to avoid infection they should not set foot outside your premises. Costs of inoculation will be around £25 per head.

POSSIBLE PROBLEMS

Meanwhile, during the foregoing period since the litter was whelped other problems may have made themselves felt. One of the more unpleasant illnesses which can effect your bitch during the time that she is feeding a litter is that of Milk Fever also known by its scientific nomenclature of Eclampsia. This is of sudden onset and, should not prompt measures be taken immediately, will probably result in the death of the bitch. It is manifested by the bitch adopting an unsteady, stiff legged gait, followed by her falling over and threshing around with her legs in a very characteristic paddling sort of style. It is quite alarming to witness, even for a seasoned breeder, accompanied as it is by a good deal of frenzied panting and eyes rolling around and unable to focus. The remedy is a single intravenous injection of calcium borogluconate which will restore matters to normal in a very short time. The cause of the illness is a sudden drop in the body's calcium and, in cattle, is habitually associated with heavy yielders. The first attack is frequently followed by further ones and it is a good precaution at the time of dosing for the initial onset of the illness to administer further massive doses of calcium borogluconate *subcutaneously* so that there is something in the nature of a reservoir of the medicine in the dog's system. Eclampsia is a disease which tends to be associated with certain animals so that a bitch which has experienced it on one occasion may be expected to go down with it at subsequent whelpings. It frequently occurs in or about the third week after parturition.

Just as there are problems such as milk fever with bitches which have a good deal of milk, there are difficulties with those which do not have enough, the effect of which is premature drying off. Apart from other considerations this is one of the reasons why it is important to start the pups on some sort of supplementary feeding at an early age as I have indicated. I have had bitches dry off at three weeks after whelping and have still reared the litters without much trouble for the reason that they have been taking other food by this time. The only difference which I have noticed in pups which have been prematurely weaned in this way, is that they always seemed to have a certain amount of difficulty in getting on with other dogs later in life. I put this down to an increased element of competitiveness having been introduced into their lives at an unnaturally early stage of their development.

A good deal worse situation than this may be encountered on those occasions when either due to the death of the dam during whelping or due to a complete cessation of her milk supply for some reason or other it is necessary to look for other means of rearing a litter. Sometimes it may be possible to foster them although this is no easy procedure even in the unlikely event of a suitable foster mother being available. Usually if you are to rear them at all in this sort of situation it is a matter of hand feeding. They will also have to be kept warm in the absence of the bitch's body heat, an air temperature of between 90° and 95°F being about right. This is best achieved with the aid of an infrared heater. If possible pups should have some of the colostrum but in any case they will require their first feed within an hour of being born. Although there are some excellent milk substitutes on the market, these may not be readily available and a good standby in an emergency of this nature is canned condensed milk. Dilute it with boiled water which has been allowed to cool in the proportions of four spoonfuls of milk to three of water. It is best given by means of a hypodermic syringe (without the needle of course) and just dripped on to the pup's tongue. Do not force the liquid in or it will get into the lungs and asphyxiate the animal. Tube feeding directly into the stomach is ideal under these circumstances but do not try it yourself. Your vet may be prepared to give you the appropriate instruction.

During the first week of their lives orphaned pups will need to be fed at three hourly intervals by both day and night. So just make sure that your alarm clock is in good working order. Newborn pups will not be able to urinate or defecate without some form of stimulation. Normally this is provided by the dam licking them but should this not be available you will have to provide the necessary stimulation by gently stroking their stomachs and genitals with a piece of towelling which has been soaked in warm water and wrung out.

Another trouble which may occur is that the bitch may contract mastitis or inflammation of the udder. This is a bacterial infection and is cured by means of a local application of antibiotics. The bitch should also be given a mild purgative such as Milk of Magnesia and hot fomentations will help in reducing the swelling.

In the event of your bitch contracting any of the illnesses which I have outlined, unless you are a very experienced dog breeder and in most cases even if you are, the wisest course will be to consult your veterinary surgeon. In fact if you are a novice breeder it will be as well if you consult your vet all along from mating to weaning, for apart from being able to shelter beneath his umbrella of superior knowledge, you will pick up a very great deal in the process which may stand you in very good stead at some time in the future, should you decide to breed again. However, by now, you may feel as many have felt before you, that this is an experience where once is enough or in some circumstances rather more than enough.

— 11 —
Lurcher Shows

To the majority of lurcher owners a show is nothing much more than a social occasion, a venue where they can meet others of similar interests and exchange views whilst engaging in a little harmless and healthy competition. A few others regard these functions as the occasion for a bit of a rave-up in the beer tent with a certain amount of swapping of tall tales regarding the abilities of their dogs. All the various claims are being put forward simultaneously so that, on the whole, no one listens to anyone else but merely keeps on talking. Thus there is little in the way of disagreement and everyone winds up feeling the better for this excursion into the world of fancy. A very small number and thank goodness it is a miniscule proportion, treat showing with deadly earnestness as though not only the entire future of their dogs but also of themselves rested upon winning. A yet smaller section are prepared to get nasty about it, frequently becoming so incoherent with fury that they are unable to discuss the matter rationally with anyone else, including the judge. By this time some of those who have been spending their time and substance in the beer tent have emerged to take part in the general disapprobation of the way in which the show is being run. Officials learn to take all these categories of competitor and non-competitor as a matter of course.

PREPARATIONS

By all means take part in lurcher shows, should your fancy take you this way. It is a good way of making friends for lurcher folk are on the whole

Enjoying the sun at a lurcher show, a great way to spend an afternoon.

friendly and outgoing so that as long as one is prepared to listen one may pick up quite a few ideas from both spectators and judges. Tidy your dog up a bit before you go and ensure that it is clean, this to include not only its coat but also its teeth and ears. Its claws should be short and free from dirt. After all a contender for the title of Miss Universe would stand little chance if seen to be sporting dirty toe nails and a lurcher show is when all is said and done a beauty contest. Watch the more seasoned of the competitors and the way in which they walk their dogs to best advantage. Generally speaking the ladies are better at this than the men. Besides perhaps treating the matter just that little bit more seriously, most of them possess a natural feminine grace to go with it, a pleasure to behold and delight to the eye.

JUDGING LURCHERS

When you go into the ring, try do do as the ring steward requests and spare a thought for this official as well as the poor old judge. They have what is often a thankless job and most of them donate their services free of charge. Judging lurchers is one of those things where a different kind of expertise altogether is required from that necessary to judge a pure breed show, and I have met one well respected judge of Whippets who confessed himself baffled on the occasion that he was kind enough to judge a lurcher show. A good deal of what goes on in a lurcher judge's mind is motivated by what may be his own personal view of what constitutes perfection, or near perfection, in lurchers. I am occasionally asked to judge at lurcher shows, and when assessing the points of the various dogs I endeavour to pick out for awards those dogs which display the various characteristics for which I would be on the look out in what I regard as a good working animal, those points which should enable it to carry out its work the better. It may be helpful if I enumerate these and they are as follows:

HEAD

The head should be long and tapering resembling that of a snake and the muzzle should be long and strong with powerful level jaws. The eyes should be set to the front of the head so that vision is to the front in the same way as that of the cheetah, lion and leopard. Ears should be small and mobile but generally carried back against the head.

NECK

Long to enable the dog to pick up with ease but at the same time muscular and strong.

SHOULDERS

Well laid back with plenty of room not less than three fingers width between the shoulder blades. This will also enhance its picking up capabilities.

BACK

Long coupled but supple with well muscled loins so as to permit a free powerful ground consuming stride similar to that of the hare. At least four fingers width between the hip bones.

CHEST

Of good depth with well spaced ribs and not too narrow but with a reasonable breadth of brisket.

HINDQUARTERS

Strongly muscled with a muscular second thigh. Plenty of length in the stifle and good angulation so as to enhance thrust. Hocks well let down for the same reason.

FORELEGS

Straight and muscular on the outer side. Flat on the inner side. Wrists well let down.

FEET

On the whole small and cat-like with well knuckled toes and short claws. However a hare foot is not penalised, nor is a let down toe which will almost certainly have been acquired during work.

COAT

Either smooth coats or broken coats or even long coats are permitted but there should be no hint of lintiness. Smooth coats should be thick and weatherproof with a dense undercoat. Its degree of weatherproofness is the yardstick.

BONE

This is judged in relation to the size of the dog and one would look for heavier bone in the larger dog with lighter bone of the Whippet type in the smaller dog.

COLOUR

I have no strong feelings about the colour of a lurcher but there are some judges who will favour a brindle dog and others who dislike a white one. As I have said I do not let a dog's colour influence me when judging lurchers, although I almost certainly would if choosing one for myself, realising at the same time that this is very much a matter of personal prejudice.

TEMPERAMENT

Lurchers are generally easy going dogs but one encounters the odd one which shows vice. If I am unable to handle any dog which I am judging, I am obviously not able to assess its true potential and am, therefore, unlikely to award it a place.

You will find that different judges have different points of view but as regards the general conformation of any dog I feel that I would be right in saying that most of us look at this in much the same way.

CLASSES

When you go to a lurcher show you will find that the various classes are organised after much the same fashion wherever you go. There are three main areas of division and these are between rough haired lurchers and smooth haired ones, between dogs and bitches, and between those animals over a certain height and those under it, this height in most cases being one of 23 inches. One goes to the odd show where the height division is at 22 inches and odd ones where the lurchers are divided by height into three categories, but these are few and far between. There is usually also a class for puppies, that is lurchers between six and 12 months of age and a class for veterans, usually confined to those over seven years old. Many shows also put on a class for a working group comprising both lurchers and terriers as well as a class for pairs. Sometimes there is a family class for a number of related animals. The latter can be very interesting indeed, always assuming that the exhibitors are not having one on, in that it may be possible to see the breeding behind a dog together with the finished result. The typical schedule therefore looks something like this:

1 Puppy 6–12 months. Rough or smooth. Dog or bitch.
2 Smooth coated dog over 23 inches.

3 Smooth coated bitch over 23 inches.
4 Rough coated dog over 23 inches.
5 Rough coated bitch over 23 inches.
6 Smooth coated dog 23 inches and under.
7 Smooth coated bitch 23 inches and under.
8 Rough coated dog 23 inches and under.
9 Rough coated bitch 23 inches and under.
10 Veterans. Dog or bitch. Rough or smooth. Seven years old and over.
11 Best matching couple. Dogs or bitches. Rough or smooth.
12 Working group. Three or more. To include at least one terrier.
13 Large lurcher champion. Winners from classes 2, 3, 4 and 5.
14 Small lurcher champion. Winners from classes 6, 7, 8 and 9.
15 Supreme lurcher champion. Winners from classes 13 and 14.

ON THE DAY

It is a good idea to arrive at the showground sufficiently early so as to leave enough time to park your vehicle and to have a look around in order to take in the general layout and geography of the place. You should also ascertain whether there is somewhere, usually a tent or a horsebox, where you have to go to enter your lurcher in such class as is appropriate to its size, sex and type of coat. It is as well at this stage if you have made yourself absolutely certain regarding its height. There should be facilities for measuring dogs on the showground but it saves time if you already know its size. Sometimes you may search in vain for any form of office where you are able to enter your dog for the reason that entries are being taken as dogs go into the ring. Having tried out both ways of taking entries, the latter is the one which I definitely prefer; it saves on the paper work and there is less in the form of tickets and receipts to lose. The ring steward simply takes each entrant's money as he enters the ring and makes a note of the rosette winners in each class as soon as it has been judged.

On the subject of entrance money, may I appeal to organisers of lurcher shows to keep this simple from the point of view of the steward having to give change. A flat fee of 50 pence or even £1 per dog gives far less hassle than fancy figures like 60 or 75 pence. Likewise as regards entry to the showground; this is best done on a basis of per car than per head and a round sum to the nearest pound is the handiest.

IN THE RING

When you go into the ring you will be expected together with the other entrants to parade your dog around for a few circuits so that the judge can see how they go and obtain an overall picture. Step out briskly and do not allow your dog to dawdle, but by the same token do not pull its head up to the extent, as is sometimes seen, of almost choking the poor brute. Keep an eye on the judge and the ring steward so that, should you be called into the centre of the ring for the judge to take a closer look at your dog, you are ready to go there. When this happens it is best not to address the judge but to speak only if spoken to, thus obviating the misgivings of other entrants who may think that you are striving to exert undue influence. The judge will probably wish to know the breeding behind the dog, if you work it and, if so, to what quarry.

PRIZES

Rosettes are usually awarded to 1st, 2nd, 3rd and 4th places these days and are red, blue, yellow and green in that order with something a bit jazzier for championship classes. Should you be awarded a 1st in one of the classes which qualifies your dog for the championship class, ensure that you remain within earshot of the ring so that you are available when the championship classes are called. If you have to leave the show before this

Bob Ward presents the trophy to Mrs Cox for her supreme champion, Scrumpy, at Molash Show on 19 August 1990 in aid of Lurcher Rescue amidst a torrential downpour.

event takes place, most officials will allow the dog to be shown by some person other than he or she who has shown it in the earlier class, so that you could leave it with some person whom you are able to trust. On the other hand, if you have to leave and take your dog along with you, it saves needless delay if you inform someone that your are doing this.

ADDED ATTRACTIONS

This is about all that there is to the normal lurcher show but there are sometimes added attractions which have been developed over the last few years, the most usual of these being lurcher racing. This is carried out over a distance of perhaps as much as half a mile over which the lurchers pursue a mechanically drawn lure consisting of a bunch of rags or a piece of fur. The dogs are organised into heats and when these have been run the winners of each heat compete against one another. This has proved to be quite a popular pastime and I have it on quite good authority that in some localities it attracts more interest than the lurcher shows themselves.

From lurcher racing other more sophisticated versions have emerged and these include speed jumping and obstacle races plus the simulated coursing which has been devised by the National Lurcher Racing Club where the lure is made to turn by means of various cunningly arranged pulleys. Often being run in parallel with such events are obedience trials and likewise a quite astonishing amount of ingenuity has gone into programming these in order to try and provide what approximates to actual working conditions.

I must confess to limited first hand knowledge about such contests. Those which I have seen, and indeed in which I have taken part upon occasion, seem to have been a success, or alternatively rather less of a success than their organisers might have wished dependent on the degree of speed and urgency or lack of them with which they were run. Nothing makes both competitors and spectators alike quite so fed up as having to spend an age between the various events and heats just waiting for something to happen. Some organisers have the happy knack of cutting out unnecessary delay so that things go smoothly with a minimum of time wasted between events. Others do not seem to possess this gift.

There is no doubt that events such as these attract a very large following, one of the best things about them being that any lurcher owner can enter his dog for any of the classes. The novice is just as welcome as the more experienced handler and all is conducted in a pleasant and friendly atmosphere. The trend of current legislation being what it is, it would only appear to be a matter of time before all forms of hunting with dogs will be banned altogether in this country. If the lurcher is then to survive it will be due to shows and other competitive activities of various kinds, and so they are to be welcomed. In this connection one can only applaud the efforts of those dedicated souls who have not only devised them but who have also worked so hard to keep them going, not the least of these being the totally committed officials of the National Lurcher Racing Club.

So go to shows by all means but do not allow yourself to forget that a lurcher is, for the time being at any rate, essentially a working dog.

Index